All About Elk

Hunter's Information Series™
North American Hunting Club
Minneapolis, Minnesota

All About Elk

Copyright© 1987, North American Hunting Club

All rights reserved.

Library of Congress Catalog Card Number 86-063878
ISBN 0-914697-07-2

Printed in U.S.A.
   12 13 14 15 16 17 18 19

Contents

Acknowledgments

The material for this book was gathered through years of experience in the field. Four of North America's best elk hunters have combined efforts to create what NAHC members demanded—the most complete elk hunting book ever written.

Their efforts were supported by the fine work of NAHC staff including Senior Vice President Mark LaBarbera, Editor Bill Miller, Associate Editor Steve Pennaz, Vice President of Product Marketing Mike Vail and Marketing Manager Linda Kalinowski.

Steven F. Burke, President
North American Hunting Club

Photo Credits

Almost all of the photographs for this book were taken by the authors. Product photos were provided by the manufacturer whose product appears in the photo. Maps, charts and graphs are credited to their source.

The Authors

Four men, each an experienced elk hunter with tremendous respect for his game, have combined their talents to provide chapters for this North American Hunting Club, Hunter's Information Series™ book. We're lucky to have the chance to benefit from this great pool of wisdom.

Mike Lapinski, Dwight Schuh, Wayne Van Zwoll and Duane Wiltse are all nationally recognized elk hunting and outfitting experts. Their scope of expertise includes biology, habitat and herd management, bow hunting, rifle hunting, guiding and outfitting, prehunt conditioning and meat care.

Mike Lapinski

Mike Lapinski, is a resident of Superior, Montana. He is a former licensed outfitter in that state and currently makes his living as a free-lance outdoor writer and photographer. His favorite subjects to cover are conservation, bow hunting, and, of course, elk hunting in general.

Mike has taken 14+ elk with archery equipment and guided hunters to even more elk with both bow and rifle. His writing and photography appear regularly in national outdoor magazines including *North American Hunter*.

Dwight Schuh

Dwight Schuh started hunting early, about age nine. But he didn't "discover" elk until the early 1970s, after his tour of duty in Vietnam. Dwight says he quickly learned the realities of elk hunting, which means he failed miserably.

From that solid beginning, he has dedicated himself to mastering what he believes is far and away North America's greatest hunting challenge. Dwight hunts primarily on his own, planning and producing his own trips.

A full-time outdoor writer and lecturer, Schuh's work regularly appears in national magazines. He has also written other books: *Bugling For Elk, Bow Hunting For Mule Deer,* and *Modern Outdoor Survival.* Dwight and his family live in Idaho.

Wayne Van Zwoll is married and makes his home in Bridgeport, Washington. He holds a master's degree in wildlife management from Oregon State University. He has worked as a range conservation officer for the Bureau of Land Management, a wildlife control and game law enforcement officer for the Washington Department of Game, and editor of *Kansas Wildlife* and *Bowhunter* magazines.

Wayne, too, is an avid elk hunter, having pursued wapiti with both gun and bow in Oregon, Wash-

Wayne Van Zwoll

ington, Idaho and Montana. He is currently a freelance outdoor writer specializing in hunting, firearms and big game of the Mountain West.

In 1971, **Duane Wiltse** gave up a prosperous mason contracting business in Flint, Michigan and moved his wife and family to an old log building ranch in the shadows of the Beartooth Mountains of northwest Wyoming.

Duane's interest in hunting is a family heritage honed for him on outdoor adventures in the peninsulas of Michigan and several Canadian provinces. Now, with more than 15 years of guiding and outfitting under his belt, Duane and his family regularly guide hunters from around the world to the trophy bull elk that inhabit the Yellowstone region west of Cody, Wyoming.

Duane Wiltse

Time permitting, Duane is active in many conservation organizations and is the author of several outdoor articles.

1

The Elk
In North America

It's supposed to be morning when these things happen; a crisp clear morning by all odds. But the sky wasn't clear, and morning was on its way out for Earl Erbes. This was the second day of Colorado's 1972 season. It was snowing and very cold.

Earl had split from his partner early, working down into mountainside timber and leaving the crest for Gary. He had cut elk tracks soon, and followed them for over two hours. Still the snow fell. It was getting deeper and Earl was thinking of turning back.

Instead he pushed on.

Each deadfall became more of a chore to crawl over; each 'pole thicket seemed a little darker. And the tracks went on. The elk would go for a long time, he knew, and each step they took covered twice as much ground as his. His sweat was freezing on him now, and his coat had that frosted look about it, especially on the shoulders, and below his chin where his breath condensed. He'd go just a little farther.

Tired now, Earl was getting clumsy, and in a particularly nasty windfall he broke a branch. It wasn't much of a branch and the snow muffled the snap. But the sound brought the elk out of their beds.

There were three of them — Earl could tell by the wink of honey-colored rump patches between snow-spattered 'poles. But then, he had known all along there were three. Three what? He saw no antlers and the elk didn't stop.

He followed them at a run, dogged their tracks through the thicket and up over a ridge and down into some more timber. His breath came hard now, but he had a feeling. When the rock rolled above him he knew it was them.

Dropping to one knee and peering under a pine branch, Earl Erbes thumbed the safety off and looked upslope. Three bulls were looking down. They were big bulls.

The crosswire wouldn't steady itself and the elk finally lost patience, whirling to plunge off through the snow. Quickly Earl jammed the reticle against the ribs of the biggest elk and fired. The bulls kept moving, all of them. He fired again. A third shot ended the hunt, and the great animal slid downhill almost to Earl's feet.

The bull's antlers would later score over 381 points, placing it in the top 15 of all the elk ever reported taken in Colorado. But Earl Erbes would remember the hunt, too; the cold and the snow and the austere 'poles, the somber sky, the expressionless granite. He'd think of tired muscles and sweat-soaked clothes and snow on his brow. He'd recall the sound of the branch snapping, the way the elk moved. He'd know forever the look of the big bovine tracks in the snow, their drag marks and kick marks. For a long time it had been just him and the tracks and the snow, and that's what he'd remember most. It had been a good hunt.

A lot of hunters today would like to get an elk like Earl's. Not very many will. It isn't that elk are in short supply; indeed, the elk population in North America is over half a million and that's five times what it was at the turn of the century. We shoot our elk hard now, though; not too many bulls live the five and six years that will give them big antlers. A few spectacular sets are collected each year, an increasing number from private land where harvest quotas are strictly enforced and expensive hunts are reserved for people who want big bulls and are willing to pay for them.

You can still get a fine elk on public land if you're willing to work for the privilege. It may take some time, and it will surely take some good planning. Not many other outdoor pursuits are as challenging as the quest for a really big elk, and few are as addicting.

Every year you hear about someone knocking off a record-book bull in his pasture or up the road in a clearcut, or stumbling onto one while he's hunting deer or changing a tire on a mountain road. Circumstances don't dictate the size of the animal, but they certainly determine how you look at elk hunting. Only the most vain and shallow fellow would consider an elk shot from roadside to be a real trophy, no matter what its score. The word trophy implies work, sacrifice, perseverence, dedication to a preset standard. Whether it's first place in a foot race or a shooting match or the achievement of some goal afield, a trophy is a prize, a reward for hardships overcome, odds beaten. You must excell to get a trophy.

That probably goes contrary to the concept most people have of trophies. But without the standard, the obstacles, the cost, the time, no prize is very meaningful. Big elk antlers are interesting objects to most hunters. They are only trophies to those who have earned them in fair chase, after paying the price. To consider any big elk a trophy without taking into account the way it was hunted and killed is to cheapen the meaning of the word. There is much to enjoy in hunting elk, and there is legitimate pride in the kill hard-won. But the joy and the pride are not a function of antler size, nor is the steel tape a measure of the hunt. Big antlers can be bought and sold; accomplishments afield cannot. There is a difference between a trophy and a souvenir.

The Origin Of Elk

Elk weren't known as elk until early colonists ran into them on the East Coast. Only vaguely familiar with the moose-like European elk, settlers were impressed by the size of the new North American animal. They named it elk because it was big like the European elk. Apparently they were unaware of our elk's relationship with the European red deer, though early writings indicate the red deer was known to some explorers. At any rate, elk became the name. Later, when the animal we know as "moose" was discovered, the whites adopted an Algonquian term, "moosh", which means "he strips bark" or "eats off." So the European elk still looks like our moose. "Wapiti", incidentally, is a Shawnee term for "white deer" or "white rump" — the origin is uncertain. For a long time, beginning around 1800, many scholars thought this the correct common name for North American elk. It is not as popular now.

Taxonomically, elk are members of the order Artiodactyla. That means even-toed animals, or ungulates. This order comprises such diverse creatures as the 10-pound mouse deer and the five-ton hippopotamus. Within Artiodactyla is the family Cervidae, which includes all antlered ruminants: 17 genera and 53 species. The genus Cervus was described by Linnaeus in 1758. It encompasses 15 species of elk-like animals in North America, Europe, Asia, the east Indies and the Phillipines. European red deer and North American elk are its two best-known representatives.

Because of the obvious physical similarities between these two animals, they were considered as one species by Linnaeus. Then in 1780 a fellow named Borowski changed the specific name of elk to *canadensis*. That decision was reversed in 1950, when several biologists argued that since red deer and elk could produce fertile offspring when crossed they should be considered as one species. They changed the name back to *elaphus*.

Elk had been in North America a few thousand years before man showed up, according to our most accurate carbon dating. Paleo-Artic Indian remains found in Alaska may be 11,000 years old, which would put them in the last of the Wisconsin glacial stage, while elk presumably inhabited Alaska as early as the Illinoian glacial stage, 120,000 years ago.

Much earlier, during the Oligocene and Miocene and Pliocene epochs, a land bridge had formed from Siberia's Chukchi Peninsula across the Bering Sea to the west coast of Alaska. Called the Bering-Chukchi Platform, this bridge or isthmus was nearly 1,000 miles wide and for some time completely exposed. During periods of maximum glaciation, the sea fell over 300 feet below its present level and many kinds of animals migrated over the platform from Asia to North America. Apparently few species from our continent moved west to Siberia.

Elk probably survived in Alaska during the Sangamonian interglacial stage, from 120,000 to 70,000 years ago. Surely they spread south and east. Later, as the Wisconsin glacier moved southward elk migrated in front of it, establishing themselves from the eastern seaboard, south of what is now Louisiana and west to the Pacific Coast. But habitat in central North America was quite different then. Spruce forests could be found in Missouri and pine uplands characterized Texas. Virginia comprised spruce parks with scattered ponds, marshes and prairies. These vegetation types were a function of glaciation: As glaciers advanced and temperatures dropped, trees spread south and west; then, during warmer, drier spells between glaciers the forests retreated to the north and east, being replaced by grasslands.

By the time the Wisconsin stage ended 10,000 years ago, spruce had disappeared from the southern plains, Paleo-Indians were hunting the sub-arctic and elk had been separated into four distinct populations. One, the largest, ranged from the Cascade and Sierra Nevada Mountains east almost to the Atlantic Coast. From the southern plains its territory extended north into what is now the Yukon. Much smaller concentrations of elk were present in central California, northern Mexico and tight to the coast in the Pacific Northwest.

Though these four major groups of elk remained more or less intact until the arrival of European man in North America, their habitat changed as the Wisconsin glacier receded. A warm, dry climate pushed the deciduous woodlands north and east, isolating them from the coniferous forests of the Mountain West. Between lay the prairies. North of them pine and juniper replaced deciduous trees and shrubs. As temperatures warmed and wildfires became more prevalent, all but the most fire-resistant woody plants were driven from the plains. Those that remained were along natural firebreaks like water courses and scarps. During this time three subspecies of elk evolved out of the largest (central) population, bringing the number of subspecies to six: Rocky Mountain elk *(Cervus elaphus nelsoni)*, Manitoban elk *(C. e. manitobensis)*, Roosevelt elk *(C. e. roosevelti)*, Tule elk *(C. e. nannodes)*, Eastern elk *(C. e. canadensis)* and Merriam elk *(C. e. merriami)*.

The Distribution Of Elk

Of the subspecies inhabiting North America when European explorers first penetrated its interior, Merriam elk were most vulnerable. Once present in Texas, New Mexico and Arizona, and in the Mexican states of Sonora, Chihuahua and Coahuila, they ranged as far south as Hidalgo and Durango, north almost to Utah. Nowhere were they plentiful. Their decline may have begun as early as the 16th century, and by the late 1800s nothing could be done to bring the animals back. The last Merriam elk was seen sometime between 1902 and 1906.

Though not officially extinct, the Eastern elk probably is. Once fairly common in the deciduous forests of the eastern U.S. and Canada, this subspecies was consumed by advancing civilization. In 1785 Pennant, in his *Arctic Zoology*, noted that elk numbers were slipping. By Audubon's time only a small section of the Allegheny Mountains supported Eastern elk.

The other four subspecies of elk are still with us, though Tule elk number less than 1,000. The Tule's range was never very great, and its habitat in the San Joaquin and Sacramento Valleys of California is now much restricted by agricultural pressures. Early explorers to California reported seeing herds of 2,000 animals, but soon competition from grazing interests and heavy shooting by meat hunters all but annihilated the elk. Agricultural development promised to finish the job. Then in 1874 a landowner named Henry Miller took an interest in the elk and established his own refuge. The handful of animals he saved became the nucleus of what is now a stable herd.

Manitoban elk, once found throughout the Great Plains from central Canada south to Oklahoma are now present only in isolated pockets in Manitoba and Saskatchewan, primarily in provincial parks. About 9,500 remain. Uncontrolled hunting was largely to blame for the decrease in herd numbers. (In 1914 Manitoba hunters reported killing 1,279 elk.) The settling of the western U.S. was instrumental as well. Though some people say elk were driven from the plains to the mountains where they

Current Distribution of Elk by Subspecies

Reproduced from **Elk of North America**, with permission from the Wildlife Management Institute.

- Manitoban elk
- Tule elk
- Roosevelt elk
- Rocky Mountain elk
- Rocky Mountain elk transplants

were better able to evade hunters, the fact is that the elk weren't driven anywhere. Those on the plains were shot, those in the mountains survived. Lots of elk — Rocky Mountain elk — were in the hills before whites started pressuring the plains animals.

Rocky Mountain elk are the most numerous of the subspecies and have always had the largest range. Much of it is remote range, too, pretty much exempt from development under current policies. From central Arizona and New Mexico north through the lower halves of British Columbia and Alberta, and from central Washington east to South Dakota, Rocky Mountain elk thrive. They have been transplanted in Florida, Pennsylvania, Michigan, Ontario, Minnesota, North Dakota, Kansas, Oklahoma, Texas, New Mexico, California and Oregon. Shot heavily during the last half of the nineteenth century, Rocky Mountain elk were scarce in the years just prior to WW I. But conservation measures have helped restore huntable numbers. Colorado, for example, allowed no elk hunting from 1903 till 1929, and the first regulated season in 1929 yielded only 895 bulls. In 1981 the Colorado Division of Wildlife sold 198,698 elk licenses!

Roosevelt elk are plentiful throughout the Coast Range and west slope of the Cascades in Oregon and Washington and can be found as far south as Humboldt County, California, as far north as Vancouver Island, B.C. Sometimes called Olympic elk, they are well established on Washington's Olympic Peninsula and have been introduced to Alaska's Afognak Island. Once Roosevelt elk roamed the hills above San Francisco, but market hunting during the gold rush days wiped them out in central California. Now, though their range has been segmented by man, these animals are on the increase in most areas where habitat is still suitable.

The American Indian And The Elk

The first elk hunters were here early. Parts of elk antlers recovered in campsites in eastern Wyoming are thought to be just over 10,000 years old. These tines were presumably used for fluting arrow and spear heads by Paleo tribes that ranged from Alberta south to New Mexico.

Paleo Indians were hunters only, primitive if resourceful people. Our knowledge of them is very limited. After them came Archaic Indians — tribes that hunted but also farmed. More adaptable than their Paleo ancestors, the Archaic peoples were also more numerous. They hunted elk too, and elk antler tools and decorations from the Archaic period have been found in Montana, Wyoming and North Dakota, as well as in excavations east of the Mississippi. The Boreal-Archaic Indians that lived 8,000 to 3,500 years ago were probably the first to hunt elk extensively. They used spears and atlatls — throwing sticks with two flint-tipped points.

By the late Archaic period, many eastern tribes were settling in villages, giving up the nomadic way of life. They remained proficient hunters, though deer figured much more heavily in their diet than elk. At one West Virginia excavation, deer remains outnumbered elk by a ratio of 34:1. At another, researchers came up with a count of 746 deer, two elk. In Pennsylvania, at a Susquehannock village, remains of 182 deer were found with those of 33 bear and 21 elk.

Fish were an important source of food for Archaic Indians in the Great Lakes country east through New England and up into Canada. Fishing spears and harpoons were often tipped with elk-antler points. These were fashioned as single or multiple barbed heads. Some heads were even equipped with toggle barbs!

As Archaic cultures evolved, farming became more important, especially to southern and eastern tribes. Elk shoulder blades were made into hoes, and tool handles were carved from elk antlers and bone. Elk also were associated with religion for these peoples. Many Archaic tribes constructed animal-shaped mounds to honor their dead, and in the upper Ohio and Great Lakes regions thousands of these mounds were built between 3,000 and 800 years ago. Though it is hard at some of these sites to distinguish the species of animal molded, elk were popular figures. One elk mound in Sauk County, Wisconsin measures more than 100 feet long and 30 feet wide!

Before Columbus, Indians had little effect on resident elk populations. Even in the West where elk were common, Indian pressure on the herds was minimal. The presence of buffalo and the limited effectiveness of Indian hunting methods throttled the take. Too, North American Indians probably numbered no more than 3.5 million by the end of the 15th century, and only 2.5 million at most lived in elk range. Elk outnumbered hunters by a big margin.

Though few tribes depended on elk for their livelihood, many prized them as game animals. In the East, Indians hunted elk by driving them into enclosures or off cliffs, shooting them from blinds by trails, snaring them with rawhide rope and following the animals in fresh snow on snowshoes. They preferred bows and spears to the first guns of white settlers. By the time firearms had become superior to more primitive weapons the Eastern elk had all but vanished.

On the Great Plains two primary Indian cultures flourished. In the arid western sections tribes were nomadic, depending almost exclusively on hunting to supply their daily needs. On the eastern prairie, where water made farming practical, Indians were more sedentary. Within these

In most cases, elk were not heavily pursued by native American Indians as a food source. There was other game more easily hunted and harvested with the Indians' primitive weapons, so they concentrated on those species. Big bulls like this were just as difficult to take back then.

two cultural divisions existed 30 major tribes and more than 30 languages. The only thing they had in common was dependence on buffalo.

To the plains Indian, elk were incidental game. They were occasionally pursued in summer because calves of the year made for much better eating than the tough meat of buffalo. Cows taken right after calving also yielded pliable hides that could be used for things not easily rendered from buffalo. Because elk were of secondary and seasonal importance, hunting them was a casual thing compared to the structured buffalo drives. The arrival of the horse made elk hunting a lot easier for most tribes, though a few, notably the Chippewa and Sarsi, considered horseback hunting for elk foolhardy. The Assiniboins hunted on snowshoes and were the only plains Indians known to use dogs in pursuit of elk. Cheyenne hunters were adept in the use of snares, while pitfalls, concealed traps and deadfalls were popular among other tribes. Blackfoot hunters drove elk toward water where the animals were easily overtaken and shot. An Oto method was to drive elk to rivers covered by thin ice. Many plains Indians waited in ambush at waterholes for elk.

Like eastern Indians, those on the prairies preferred their bows over the first firearms for big game. The exposed locks of early muzzle-loaders were unreliable, ammunition hard to come by. Smoothbore muskets scarcely had greater effective range than a bow and made a lot of noise.

In the mid-19th century when breech-loading single-shots became available they were prized for all kinds of hunting, though the precious ammunition was often saved for buffalo and bluecoats. By the time repeating rifles came along, elk were almost gone from the grasslands. For these reasons guns were probably very little used by plains Indians for hunting elk, early or late.

Southwestern Indians were primarily farmers, supplementing their produce with wild plants, rabbits, deer and pronghorns. Those who did hunt elk generally stalked them, killing with bows and arrows or spears. Throwing sticks and clubs were used too, and often the hunters dressed in animal skins to avoid detection. Some California Indians, notably the Yana, ambushed elk at salt licks. The Maidu and Konkow drove elk to concealed hunters or stalked them or actually chased them down. Elk driven to rivers were overtaken as they swam, caught by the legs, and their throats slashed. The Chimarikos used converging fires to trap and kill big game, while the Nomlakis ran down their prey in relays. The Wintu hunted elk on snowshoes; the Yuki set snares on trails; the Karoks and other tribes used dogs to herd elk into ravines and deep pits.

To the north, in the Coast and Cascade Ranges, large groups of Chinnook, Clatsop and Tillamook Indians drove elk toward snares, pits and deadfalls. Dogs were often used. The Bella Coola, Nootka and Kwakiutl Indians sometimes made big nets of sinew and stretched them across trails just before a drive. Entangled, the elk were caught and killed. Indians around Puget Sound chased elk to water, then clubbed them or shot them from canoes. Spears (gigs), bows and arrows and metal-tipped clubs were popular with Pacific Coast natives; the cheap Hudson Bay muskets brought in as trade guns were little more effective.

For Columbia River tribes salmon were 80 percent of the diet. These people didn't hunt very often. Farther inland, away from the rivers and as far north as the southern Yukon, Indians killed elk when they could. When white traders penetrated the interior and put a premium on elk teeth, hides and meat the Indians hunted harder. Both the Northern Athapaskan and Central Algonquin tribes preferred caribou and moose for domestic purposes.

Elk teeth, especially the canine tusks, were highly regarded as decorations by many tribes. Teeth have been found at village sites dating back nearly 5,000 years, and in the late 19th century 100 tusks would buy a horse. Usually drilled then sewn on both men's and women's garments, tusks were also strung on necklaces or worn as pendants, displayed on shields, medicine pouches, dog harnesses. By the time elk became scarce some Indians had acquired the skill of making artifical tusks of bone. Reportedly they could not be told from the real thing.

Elk antlers were used by Indians for making war clubs, arrow straighteners, saddle trees, spears, harpoons, gaffs, even bows. A bow could be fashioned from one long antler, shaved thin and backed with sinew, or it could comprise four slivers of antler, two glued back-to-back to form one limb, then joined in a section of solid antler to the other limb. Antler bows apparently didn't last very long. Tools and utensils made from antlers fared better and quite a few specimens survive. Antlers were occasionally used for decoration but were not considered trophies as we think of trophies today. In several places elk antlers (mostly winter sheds) were gathered and piled into tall mounds. Some approached 20 feet in height, with base diameters of 15 feet. Nobody knows yet what these antler heaps mean.

Elk bones were used to make needles, awls and forks, as well as small specialized tools. Bones could also be boiled to produce a tallow better than that rendered from fat. After the white conquest of the prairies, elk bones were scavenged, along with those of buffalo, by reservation Indians. They swapped them at trading posts for canned meat. Shipped east, bones brought $4 to $30 a ton. One writer of the period estimated that the bones of big game salvaged on the prairie for transport east would fill a string of freight cars 7,575 miles long — enough to stretch from San Francisco to New York and back.

Most Indians that lived on buffalo meat liked it. They didn't like elk as well. Elk meat spoiled quicker than buffalo — though the Carrier Indians deliberately let their meat sour to improve its taste. If elk had a bad reputation among some tribes it was because they only hunted elk when no other food was to be had: in the dead of winter when animals were losing weight and only the weakest were vulnerable. Unlike bison, elk was often eaten raw. It if was cooked, it was boiled. A lot of Indians thought cooking drew strength from the meat.

Elk jerky was, like buffalo jerky, a staple of hunting tribes. Sun-cured or smoked, the lean meat weighed about 80 percent less when dry and kept almost indefinitely. Fat in equal proportions was mixed with pulverized jerky to form pemmican, which could be cut into cakes. "Summer pemmican" made of buffalo would keep for several years. "Winter pemmican", a moister food often made of elk and containing berries as well as meat, had a shorter lifespan but was much more palatable and nutritious.

Elk skin was traditionally used as cold weather and ceremonial wear by plains Indians and those in the Mountain West. In some cultures elk hide was worn only by men, but in others it was a symbol of wealth for both men and women. It also served as sole material for stout, knee-length moccasins. Leggings were made of elk, as were shield covers, the shield itself being of horse or buffalo hide, double thick. Nez Perce and Shoshone warriors made shields from two layers of elk rawhide, usually of the necks of bulls. Some Indians, Blackfeet in particular, preferred to darken their elk leather through a smoking process.

Most Indian tepee covers were of buffalo hide or, in the north, moose. Cree, Kutenai and Northern Shoshones used elk for this purpose, though. Belts, harnesses, bedding, pouches, ropes, scabbards, quivers, even canoes were of elk. Like the buffalo, the elk was a part of Indian culture, a resource tapped to meet the needs of daily life, a creature to share the land. It was killed, respected, used, worshipped. It wasn't sold until the whites came.

Lewis and Clark found that Indians on the upper Missouri commonly traded elk skins. But commerce in elk was brought later by the settlers. When the cartridge rifle became available to the Indian, hunting for market replaced subsistence hunting as a way of life. The attitude of man toward animal changed, and it was this as much as white hostility that compromised the red man's independence. The U.S. Army hurried things along, but the shift in perspective evidenced by indiscriminate killing for market would have been tragic had the Indians been free to pursue it into the 20th century.

With the completion of the transcontinental railroad, the capacity to ship exceeded the abilities of Indians to kill and deliver elk. White profiteers found elk shooting a lucrative prospect, especially when the supply of buffalo ran low. They encouraged and sometimes hired Indians to kill game. Wintering elk were especially vulnerable. In the winter of 1869-70 in an area 15 miles square in northwest Wyoming over 4,000 elk were shot. Only the hides and tongues were taken from most of them.

For most of the market hunting era that spanned the 1870s hides were the most marketable part of elk and buffalo. Meat was difficult to process and ship, so little was used. Buffalo hides brought about $4 each at railhead, elk about $7. The average annual per capita income was only $170. As late as 1881, when most of the buffalo had been shot and the elk had dwindled alarmingly, 5,000 market hunters and skinners still prowled the Mountain West.

As with other animals, elk shot by Indians before the settling of the frontier were almost totally consumed. The hooves of an elk were boiled for glue, its stomach and other internal organs made into pouches, its hair used for decoration, its sinews for making thread and bowstrings.

In early autumn just before the rut, bachelor groups of bulls are still together. Soon the bulls will be jousting, bugling, wallowing in mire wet with their own urine. They'll eat little, relying on energy from fat stored in the liver. These bulls are fine specimens of today's Rocky Mountain elk.

Nothing was wasted in the early times because elk were hard to hunt and kill. When the white men made it easy, things changed.

Physiology

Though six subspecies of elk are recognized, they don't differ all that much in physical appearance. Antler conformation, body size and coat color are the most noticeable variables, but these can vary within a subspecies in different parts of its range too.

The most distinct elk is the Roosevelt. Antlers in Roosevelt bulls are generally heavier for their length than antlers of other subspecies and tend to "crown" or grow a number of points at odd angles at the last fork in the main beam. In this respect they are a lot like the European red deer. The Roosevelt's antlers and coat are darker than those of other subspecies, though Manitoban elk are dark too.

Body weight varies within populations and according to forage conditions, but the subspecies rank in size from heaviest to lightest like this: Merriam elk, Roosevelt elk, Manitoban elk, Rocky Mountain elk, Tule, elk. No records are available for Eastern elk, and the size of Merriam elk is largely postulated from the size of its skull. Of the existing four species, Tule elk are the smallest, a large bull weighing 500 to 600 pounds. Rocky Mountain and Manitoban elk are close in size, a mature bull scaling 750 to 800 pounds. Roosevelt elk are larger by about 100 pounds.

These are generalizations, and elk of any of the heavier three subspecies may weigh over 1,000 pounds. Bulls this big, though, are exceptional.

A mature Rocky Mountain bull stands right at five feet at the shoulder. Its front legs are up to three feet long, its total length about 7½ feet. Its lung volume roughly equals its blood supply: six gallons. Its heart may weigh nine pounds. The resting pulse rate of an adult male is 70 beats per minute. Pulse rate for bulls is about 25 percent higher than that of cows.

All elk have 34 teeth: three lower incisors, an upper and lower canine, three upper and three lower premolars, three upper and three lower molars per side. The lower canines are not nearly as prominent as the tusks above.

The digestive system of elk is common to all ruminants. It comprises four compartments: *rumen, reticulum, omasum* and *abomasum.* The abomasum is the true stomach and last in line. An elk's rumen is not functional at birth but, with the reticulum, develops rapidly until the animal is about a year old. *At that time it is large enough to hold almost 40 percent of the body weight in forage!* At maturity that figure is closer to 20 percent.

The rumen, three-chambered, contains microorganisms that permit the elk to digest cellulose, something a single-stomached animal cannot do. Rumen pH in elk is about 6.3. Rumen material is regurgitated in a bolus, chewed again and reswallowed. Elk usually chew their cud long after feeding and while bedded in a safe place.

A bolus that has been thoroughly chewed is directed through a chamber-like organ called the atrium from the esophagus to the reticulum. The reticulum has a mucous membrane inside that divides its walls into a honeycomb of compartments. The next pouch, the omasum, is a muscular organ with a rough inside that, when contracted, can squeeze a lot of readily-absorbed liquid out of the forage. Once this is done the food passes into the abomasum and is handled pretty much like it would be in a single-stomached animal.

Elk are adaptable feeders and can digest grasses, forbs and woody plants with minimal acclimatization. They definitely prefer grasses and forbs, which may comprise 85 percent of their diet in late fall and early spring. Browse generally constitutes 20 to 40 percent, is most palatable in early spring but most often eaten in winter when little else is to be had. Forbs account for over 20 percent of the diet in early summer and fall, the only times they're readily available in quantity. The daily intake of dry meadow grass for a mature elk ranges from 1.7 to 2.9 pounds per hundred pounds of body weight. That's 12 to 18 pounds a day for a big bull!

An elk liver is capable of some pretty strange things. It stores vitamin

It's raining, but this sleek bull doesn't mind. As long as the forage and cover are adequate he can weather severe extremes of climate. His body actually uses more energy to stay cool in summer than warm in the winter. He can survive wind chills 150 degrees below body temperature!

A all right, and produces glycogen just like livers everywhere. But during early rut the bull elk's liver accepts a lot of lipids (fats and sterols) from other parts of the body. These are accumulated, raising the fat content of the liver to almost 50 percent! The fat changes the liver color from deep red to yellow or pink. In this way a bull has a ready supply of easily-metabolized fat and can undergo prolonged fasting during rut.

Elk aren't all the same color. Season, habitat, subspecies, age and sex all seem to play a part in determining color. After the spring molt elk are relatively dark, an even brown tending toward chestnut. Legs and belly are darker, almost black. As the summer passes and fall arrives the torso lightens. The rump patch remains a pale tan or yellow; the legs stay dark; the head and neck may become a deeper brown. In fall bulls are generally — *certainly not always* — lighter than cows. If you're looking for antlers among a group of elk it's best to check out the lightest-colored first. Old bulls may be almost white. As with deer, elk in forested habitat seem to be darker than elk in open country.

Antler growth in elk, as in all cervids, orginates from a pedicel in the skull. Growth is prompted by changes in photoperiod and may begin as early as January. The growing period for antlers is 90 to 140 days, depending on size. By the middle of August the core of the antler has hardened, the blood vessels supplying life to the velvet have shriveled and the velvet begins to peel off the bone in strips. The bull hastens this process by rubbing his antlers on trees and bushes. Velvet is shed about the same time on spikes and mature bulls. The older animals start growing antlers sooner, however.

A lot of people used to think rubbing was done to scratch antlers because they itched. But by the time the velvet splits on the bone, the core is very hard, the velvet nothing but dead tissue. When the core is actively growing, the velvet has very sensitive nerve endings as well as apocrine and sweat glands, but once the antler is mature, it's unlikely any feeling is left in this temporary skin. The rubbing may be a pre-rut activity, but is often done quite a long time before the rut and before the bull shows any interest in cows.

The freshly-cleaned antlers are dead bone, comprising of about 22 percent calcium and 10 percent phosphorous. Water content is between 40 and 50 percent, air-dry weight 80 percent of actual weight. The antlers are firmly attached throughout the rut. In fierce struggles with other elk a bull may break a main beam or crack his skull near the antler base but will not lose the antler at the point of connection.

Because testosterone levels play a major part in antler growth, not all bulls drop their antlers at the same time. Bulls that have been sexually relaxed since October may shed in January, but one that has

Judging elk antlers is difficult. This is a nice bull and would easily qualify for the Pope & Young list. The 375-point Boone & Crockett minimum, though, is a much higher hurdle.

experienced delayed rut may retain his antlers well into March. The antlers usually drop cleanly, having been separated from the pedicel by the resorption of tissue on its top layer.

Antlers get bigger as bulls get older, up to an age of seven or eight. At this point a lot depends on diet and genetics. Pedicel size determines antler diameter and each year as the bull matures his pedicels become shorter and broader. The bony cap on the pedicel after shedding is convex. When the elk reaches old age or comes upon hard times this cap will be flat, indicating a plateau in antler development. A concave cap means the animal will probably have smaller antlers the next year than he had last and that he is in deteriorating health.

Most elk have spike antlers their first season. Branch-antlered yearlings occur quite often where genetics and diet are favorable. The second-year bull is usually a raghorn, with branched antlers that may have from three to six points but commonly five. Healthy elk in good habitat are six-points as three-year-olds, and many retain this number of tines through their fourth and subsequent seasons, simply adding weight and length each year. Seven-point bulls are much less common than six-points, but are not rare. Elk with eight points or more per side *are* rare, but occur most frequently in populations of Roosevelt elk. The extra tines generally grow from the crown at the last antler fork. Antlers on mature bulls can scale up to eight percent of the animal's dressed weight.

The Pope and Young minimum score for Rocky Mountain elk is 240, for Roosevelt elk 210. Boone and Crockett bulls must measure 375 and 290 for the book. If you hunt elk a lot you'll likely see a few animals that would make the P&Y list, but you won't see many that meet B&C criteria. A record-book bull will look big! You'll have no doubts. The elk you wonder about, the one you think just might make the minimum, probably won't.

Life Cycle

Elk rut from mid-September to early October in most of their range. In healthy populations the active rut may be as short as three weeks, with most receptive cows being bred by dominant bulls in that time. But because many elk populations have a shortage of mature bulls, or if hunting pressure or weather disrupts the rut, cows may not be fertilized on schedule. A cow's receptive period is only 12 to 18 hours long. If she isn't bred during this time she'll come into estrus again 21 days later. A third estrus is common, a fourth possible but unlikely. So breeding in unbalanced elk populations may go on for up to nine weeks.

Neither female nor male elk can breed successfully as calves though both can do so as yearlings. Pregnancy rates from yearling cows vary from zero to 100 percent. Where large bulls are available for breeding, spike bulls do little actual fertilization. Often they are even tolerated in the herds during the rut, when dominant bulls are chasing off raghorns. Yearling bulls may even be allowed to mount cows. Possibly the activity of yearling males serves as a stimulus to ready the cows.

The best breeding years for cows are ages three through seven, when pregnancy rates generally average over 90 percent. Bulls of about the same age group are the best breeders because they are the most virile and active then, with fully developed antlers and the strength to assert their dominance. Though it appears that the herd bull chooses, wins and keeps a harem, the lead cow probably selects the harem master on the basis of his strength, size and sexual displays. Either way, the biggest, most aggressive bull is apt to do most of the breeding in any given herd.

While bull elk in the wild usually don't live long enough to become impotent, the reproductive capability of cows declines after age seven. Only about half the cows seven to 10 years old conceive and those 11 or older are generally sterile.

Bulls advertise themselves during the rut by bugling, horning, wallowing, rubbing and urinating on themselves. Deep, hoarse bugles come from the older bulls and are a sign of strength and masculinity to cows. Horning trees and shrubs and jousting with other bulls demonstrate aggression and dominance. Wallowing and rubbing and urinating are often done together, the bull urinating first on his belly, even through his front legs onto his neck. He then rolls in a wallow or mud hole, emerging to rub his neck on a nearby tree. Saturated with mud and urine, he's ready to court or fight!

The gestation period for elk is 247 to 262 days. Single calves are the rule; twins occur less than one percent of the time. Newborn elk weigh 23 to 45 pounds, with males scaling about four pounds more than females. After giving birth around June 1 the cow will nurse her calf for 2½ months. During this time calf mortality may exceed 50 percent, nearly all of it occurring the first three weeks of life. Malnutrition and predation by bears and coyotes are the most significant factors. Mountain lions figure heavily in some areas. Add a hard winter and yearling mortality may reach 80 percent!

Mortality among elk older than a year is caused primarily by environmental factors and hunting. Predators take some elk, as do natural accidents and diseases. Among the major bacterial diseases of elk are actinomycosis, anthrax, arthritis, brucellosis, clostridia, leptospirosis, necrotic stomatitis. These cause few deaths in wild elk populations and are not usually as severe a problem as parasites. Elk host ticks, mites (including the scab mite), lice, flukes, tapeworms, roundworms and parasitic protozoa. Infestations can be severe. Two Roosevelt elk calves determined to die of lungworm complications were found to contain 9,287 and 18,567 gastrointestinal roundworms as well!

Habitat

The wet forests of the Olympic Peninsula differ markedly from the juniper hills of Arizona, but elk are found in each place. While habitat preferences vary as widely as the vegetation in elk areas, some are common to most native elk range.

Summering in high country where cool breezes and shade abound, elk eat forbs and grasses as long as they remain palatable. About the middle of July, when open areas begin to dry up and the nutritional value of forage declines, elk take to the timber, seeking out plants in earlier, more lush stages of growth. Autumn frosts generally trigger a switch to shrubs.

Scattered in small bands and bachelor groups for most of the summer, elk form harems for the rut, then break up again and regroup later for fall migration. Early snows don't have much of an effect on them, but even a light dusting in November can prompt a mass exodus of the high country. The elk then move down to a transition zone, usually comprising of ponderosa pine/Douglas-fir or mixed conifer forests at middle elevations. Hunting seasons may hold the elk in the most inaccessible parts of this range until snow drives them to the valleys.

Even in winter elk don't like to stay on drainage bottoms. They much prefer slopes, and the upper half of slopes at that. Whenever they can, they'll spend winter days on a south slope or a ridge, up where the sun melts the snow off the grass and the wind sweeps fresh snow away. Cold weather is no problem for elk. With thick hide and a heavy coat of hollow winter hair, they can survive wind chills of over 150 degrees below body temperature and buck two feet of snow with relative ease. Forage is the critical factor. If the winter range is in good shape and provides snow-free feeding areas and a little thermal cover, elk thrive in the bitterest weather. In fact, they spend more energy keeping cool in summer than warm in winter!

Come spring the elk retrace their steps to the high country, stopping in the forested transition zone long enough to taste its most succulent victuals, just uncovered. This new growth is a welcome change from the dry grass and browse of late winter's diet. As melting snow permits, the bulls head for the slopes above. Elk don't like really steep country, though they'll use it to escape hunters or travel through it from one drainage to the next. Most elk activity is on slopes of 20 percent

A happy hunter with as nice a bull as you're likely to find most places these days. If you want to land one high in the B&C list, consider that in the last 20 years only two bulls have made the top 30!

or less, and very little foraging occurs on slopes steeper than 50 percent.

Pregnant cows split from migrating bands of elk in the transition zone. There they seek cover and solitude and have their young. Several days to several weeks later each cow will join with other cows and move upslope with her calf.

Elk As A Resource

From a high point in the early 1800s, elk populations in North America were shot to dangerously low levels in the last years of that

Forty Years of Elk Hunting Data, Western U.S. and Canada

	Elk License Sales	Reported Elk Kill	Percent Hunter Success
1979	755,179	103,781	14
1978	730,380	104,132	14
1977	656,869	109,722	17
1976	621,265	81,888	13
1975	630,999	103,830	16
1974	649,487	93,323	14
1973	637,771	109,225	17
1972	530,960	86,735	16
1971	510,041	80,861	16
1970	538,455	95,675	18
1969	504,963	93,128	18
1968	490,073	96,327	20
1967	432,540	83,868	19
1966	432,509	90,907	21
1965	412,872	77,334	19
1964	400,876	87,900	22
1963	345,819	85,058	25
1962	335,666	68,800	20
1961	312,393	68,398	22
1960	292,563	73,837	25
1959	287,224	67,888	24
1958	270,723	65,474	24
1957	249,274	58,470	23
1956	256,527	65,025	25
1955	237,723	67,454	28
1954	164,029	54,939	33
1953	157,839	52,885	34
1952	192,711	38,118	20
1951	189,451	56,104	30
1950	167,388	55,754	33
1949	158,230	51,501	33
1948	106,778	44,193	41
1947	93,132	30,087	32
1946	80,764	37,356	46
1945	54,030	19,020	35
1944	28,120	12,907	46
1943	36,985	21,491	58
1942	20,556	8,078	39
1941	29,642	8,686	29
1940	20,379	8,254	40

Data compiled from **Elk of North America**, used with permission from the Wildlife Management Institute.

century. Little was done to conserve elk or any other big game. They were simply animals to be killed for profit and food.

By the late 1880s, though, it became apparent that wildlife was not a permanent fixture. The buffalo, once so numerous that over-harvest seemed an absurd idea, were almost gone. Elk were very scarce. Conservationists like Theodore Roosevelt took action to save what was left. In 1887 Roosevelt formed the Boone and Crockett Club, an organization not for the purpose of record-keeping — that came later — but to combat the exploitation of big game.

Strict protective measures in the first two decades of the 20th century helped stabilize declining game populations. By the late twenties hunting was being allowed where seasons had been closed for years. By the 1930s most states had staffed their own wildlife agencies. As certainly as the market hunters of the 1870s had devastated elk herds, sport hunters led the way in bringing the animals back. Teddy Roosevelt's motives for his conservation efforts weren't political; they were real, based on a personal concern for wildlife he acquired on the hunting trail. So it was with most of the other conservationists who have since given of their time and money to improve the lot of all wildlife.

Were it not for hunters today, game agencies would immediately run out of funds. Scientific investigations, habitat development, transplanting would cease. Damage control on farm and forest would become a function of the landowner, who would be free to destroy problem wildlife without answering to the public. Our knowledge of and, consequently, interest in wildlife would wane. Land development would take precedence over land conservation; critical habitats would be destroyed. When no one cares about a resource it is accorded no care, no budget! It is ignored, bled slowly by other priorities that conflict with its survival.

Elk have a price now, and they will as long as they're hunted. Even people who have no feeling for wildlife can understand economics, and elk contribute a lot of money to states where they're hunted. In 1980, for example, over 755,000 U.S. and Canadian elk hunters bought licenses, paying a total of $25.3 million just for their tags! The amounts spent by these hunters on food, lodging, gasoline, arms, ammunition and camp supplies and outfitter fees can only be estimated, but it's interesting to note that in *one Kansas county* the first weekend of *pheasant* season bird hunters contribute over a quarter million dollars annually to the local economy through purchased services!

Annual elk harvest for the western U.S. and Canada now exceeds 100,000 animals. Colorado is perennially the top state. In 1979 it led with 27,871 animals. Wyoming was a distant second with 18,580. Oregon's hunters took 16,128, Washington's 12,270, Montana's 11,692, Idaho's 6,344.

Today, elk hunting is much more than just shooting an elk. It's the country and the season, the men and the horses, the silence and the smells, and the taste of camp cooking. It's the creak of leather, the oil-slick slide of your rifle bolt. It's a call that brings you back again and again.

Of the elk licenses bought in 1980, 11 percent were by non-resident hunters. That figure will increase, despite rising fees, in the future. Crowding will increase too, as will pressure on elk herds that already have too few mature bulls left after hunting season to breed the cows over the next rut. To combat these problems some states, notably Montana and Idaho, are limiting the number of non-resident tags they sell. Other agencies, like Colorado's, have split elk season into short segments to spread pressure, relegating each hunter to his choice of one period. Many states, like Oregon, have adopted "either-or" strategies for primitive weapons hunters. You may hunt there with a rifle or bow but not both, and the seasons are separate. Washington sells its tags by unit; you may hunt only one. Many states have designated areas with specific antler point restrictions to reduce the take of yearling bulls.

Because more and more hunters are clamoring for the chance to shoot a mature bull, western game agencies are changing their management strategies. Areas are now being set aside where only mature bulls are legal game. These are generally permit-only units, with the number of hunters limited to preserve hunt quality. In effect, hunters are now being forced to choose between management that will offer the most chances to shoot an animal and management that offers fewer chances at bigger animals. Whichever way states decide to go, more restrictive hunting — shorter seasons, more permit-only units, higher license fees — is in the offing. Under the trophy concept it will just get here quicker.

The prognosis for trophy elk hunting is good. Trophy-class bulls will still be available — in fact, they may well become more available! The chances for a really big bull will be greatest where big bulls have been taken before. These aren't necessarily areas with the highest elk concentrations or hunter success rates. Indeed, the opposite is often true. They are areas that are remote, with excellent elk habitat. They are hard to hunt, and because they are hard to hunt bulls get older there.

The problems with trophy hunting won't come from the field. Anti-hunters will continue to actively oppose sport hunting, but especially trophy hunting. Their proposals would remove the price tag from our game animals and in so doing guarantee its doom. Often well-intentioned, these people have little understanding of the ways of nature, the history of game management, the needs of wildlife today. Emotional, they will strike out in any way they can. Frustrated, they will turn our own statements against us if they can.

There is little danger the anti-hunters can win substantial ground with their own devices. But they're smart enough to spot holes in logic no matter how foreign the subject. They will continue to attack trophy hunters as egotistical buffoons, intent on self-glorification through the death of another creature. No matter that hunting itself is a proven game management technique; if we participate because we want to feed egos, that will be used against us by people who can argue persuasively that in our society motive *does* matter, that wild game is not like beef, to be hammered in a chute for meat alone.

If you're an elk hunter, you know there *is* more afield than an opportunity to salt away a winter's meat. But if you can't describe it to the uninitiated you'll have a hard time convincing anyone you should be out in the woods, or that hunters are any more sophisticated, mentally, than they were when they systematically wiped out entire populations of game.

Meat, antlers and camaraderie are all legitimate gains from a day or a week in the woods, but the challenge is what makes it a hunt. If the elk you shot is to mean anything, the way you hunted it and shot it is important. It needn't have a place in the book to be a trophy to you, but it must have been hunted. Big antlers can be bought as souvenirs, and supermarket beef is cheaper than venison. You can see the boys any time. But only on a hunt can you pursue a trophy animal. If you explain that to people who've never hunted they probably won't understand you, but if you don't they certainly will.

Backpacking for elk is a very rewarding way to hunt. When you've bagged a big bull you know you've earned it. Overall, hunter success has dropped from a high of around 50 percent just before World War II, to about 14 percent today.

2

Planning a
Self-Guided Hunt

It's one thing to dream about roaming the high, wild, and lonesome on your own, footloose and free as a mountain man. It's another to place yourself in the realities of mountain life and come out with the same self-respect and enthusiasm you started with. Most elk country, and the elk themselves, can disillusion you quickly if you're not prepared.

Why is elk hunting tough? Co-author of this book, Mike Lapinski, a member of the North American Hunting Club who lives in Montana, has guided elk hunters and also has helped nonresidents plan their own elk hunts. One year he helped three experienced hunters from Wisconsin plan a bowhunt for elk during the bugling season. These hunters had all taken several deer and bear apiece, so they were hardly novices, yet they came away from their elk hunt discouraged.

One obstacle that exceeded their greatest imagination was the physical demands of western hunting. Even though they all had been running and lifting weights to prepare, they found their conditioning woefully inadequate. In talking to other hunters, particularly those from the East who have never hunted big mountains at high elevations, I found that reaction to be widespread.

Lapinski's friends also had difficulty adapting to the nature of the elk themselves. They had read extensively about elk, but they still didn't understand the habits of elk and had a tough time locating animals. And when they did find bugling bulls, they didn't know what to do with them. Elk hunting bore few similarities to the deer and bear hunting they had

Many novice elk hunters underestimate the physical demands. If you can't handle prolonged exertion in steep terrain, the self-guided hunt may not be for you.

perfected back home. The average hunting success in Montana is about 15 percent, but one of the Wisconsin hunters, after his initial elk expedition, said he would give the beginner on his own a zero to one percent chance of success.

I believe your chances are better than that, but the experience of those hunters does point out one important fact: The self-guided elk hunt is not for everyone. You must be a special breed of cat to make it work.

Test Yourself

How do you know if you're the man—or woman—to take on elk hunting by yourself? To answer that question, examine yourself. Some hunters have the ability to fare for themselves and others don't, and there's no sense in kidding yourself. Evaluate your own abilities honestly.

First how dear are time and money to you? If you're short on time and long on money, planning your own hunt is probably counterproductive. Self-planning takes time, and if you don't have time to spare, hiring an outfitter could be cheaper.

Outfitted hunts are often viewed as expensive undertakings, but when you consider the horses, transportation, camping gear, and other expenses attendant any serious elk hunting, you find that outfitting yourself isn't cheap. If you plan to hunt elk every year, the expense may be justified, but if you'll hunt elk only once or twice in your lifetime, the money you would pour into equipment would be largely wasted.

Physical ability plays a big part, too. Hunting on your own requires considerable physical demands in setting up your equipment, hiking miles on foot, handling your own game, cooking for yourself after a long day in the field. If you're a vigorous person who thrives on exertion, then you'll probably do well on your own, but if that's not appealing, then you'll fare better with an outfitter who'll supply a horse for you to ride, butcher and pack your game, have meals prepared at night, and so forth.

Planning your own elk hunt takes a certain amount of initiative and research, and to do that you must be a self-starter, the kind of person who thrives on doing things for himself. If you're easily discouraged or frustrated when things go awry, you'll have a hard time on your own as an elk hunter. On the other hand, if you thrive on challenge and can turn defeats into victories, then you're probably cut out for self-guided elk hunting.

You don't have to have experience with elk to hunt these animals successfully, but a fundamental knowledge of woodcraft, outdoor lore, and wildlife are essential. If you know your way around the woods, know how to read sign, spot animals and stalk, have done some game calling and so forth, then you probably can adapt quickly to Western conditions and can hunt elk well. But if you've had little hunting experience and plan to take on elk as your first quarry, do it with an outfitter who has the needed lore.

Define Your Goals

Once you decide you're qualified to hunt on your own, the dreaming ends and the planning begins. Research is the secret word. If you do your homework, odds are you'll have a great trip. If you simply head to the mountains on a prayer, hoping things will work out, chances are overwhelming that Murphy's law will get the best of you.

Before you can do any meaningful research, you have to know what you expect from a hunt. Business efficiency counselors advise, "You can't get somewhere unless you know where you're going. So set some goals." If that's true for businessmen, it's equally true for hunters. You must know what you want before you can plan for it.

First, what kind of an elk are you looking for? Will you settle for nothing less than a 6-point bull? Will any bull regardless of size satisfy you? Would you be happy shooting any kind of elk, including a cow?

Do you insist on an area with lots of elk, or would you settle for fewer elk as long as you can enjoy some solitude and beautiful scenery? Do you want to bugle a bull, or would you prefer to track him in snow? Do you want to backpack, horse camp, or car camp? Are you looking for easy access or wilderness?

Brainstorm with your hunting partners and write down all your ideas. Keep at it until you've built a composite picture of the ideal hunt. Now you've got some basis for further planning.

Hunting Modes

Buying Your Own Horses. In the minds of many hunters, elk and wilderness go together. Long-distance wilderness hunting, say more than five miles from the road, requires horses or other pack animals. Some hunters who hunt elk year after year find buying their own horses worthwhile. Many keep their horses at home and trailer them to the hunting area, but others find it simpler and probably cheaper to pasture their horses with a rancher near the hunting area. The use of horses for back-country hunting is a specialized subject beyond the scope of this chapter, but it's a workable alternative if you plan to hunt elk seriously.

The Drop Camp. For most hunters, this may be the best all-around option for self-guided wilderness hunting. You either can hire an outfitter to set up a camp for you, using his equipment and gear, or you can have him drop off your own camping gear at a predetermined location.

Even drop-camp hunts demand planning. If you rely strictly on a

Some hunters who go after elk every year, find it worthwhile to buy their own horses. You can keep them at home and trailer them to your hunting area, or you can board them with a local rancher.

packer to choose the location, you could find yourself in a bad spot. He may have a number of drop camps, and you could find yourself in a crowd, even in the wilderness. Or if the outfitter is running guided hunts at the same time, he may stick you in a second-rate location. Obviously, he'll take his guided hunters into the prime country. For these reasons, you're wise to pick your own location (I'll detail research methods later) and to tell the packer where you want your camp.

In addition, make sure services are clearly outlined. A friend of mine arranged a drop camp, and the outfitter agreed to set up tents and tables, and to provide stoves, lanterns, gas and other needed accessories. When my friend arrived in camp, 17 miles from the nearest road, he found no white gas. He spent several days in the dark, cooking over a campfire.

In another case, I killed a deer early in a hunt. The outfitter, as prearranged, showed up at the end of the first week to pack out the meat. He promised to place the deer in cold storage. When we emerged from the backcountry at the end of two weeks, I found my deer still hanging at air temperature at the outfitter's base camp, the meat molding badly.

In another situation, an outfitter quoted me a price of $100 to pack out an elk. After I had killed a bull, the price suddenly jumped to $400. Naturally I about exploded. The outfitter patiently explained that he had been talking about a different area. My elk was in a rough spot, much farther from the road than he had anticipated, so he had to charge me more. Make sure before you ever set out that the details of a hunt are clearly understood by both parties.

Backpacking is an inexpensive way to hunt elk, but quarters are cramped and the amount of gear you can take with you is limited.

Backpacking. Regardless of the hunting mode, you'll pay dearly for a backcountry hunt. To hire a packer you pay in money; to backpack you pay in energy. My friend Larry Jones, during a week-long backpack hunt in Montana, well expressed the reaction you may feel in backpacking for elk.

"Why do we do stuff like this? Why don't we just hunt off the road like everyone else?" Larry groaned as we slumped to the ground to relieve our bodies from the burden of heavy packs.

"Maybe we're crazy," I replied.

"Maybe, nothing," Larry sighed.

That's probably not an atypical reaction among backpacking elk hunters. Sometimes it hardly seems worth the effort. On the other hand, backpacking gives you excellent mobility, and the achievement of doing it all yourself offers satisfaction that few other forms of hunting can match. I've backpacked for elk many times for as long as two weeks, and I've enjoyed some excellent hunting.

However, backpacking has its limitations. If you envision saddling yourself up with two weeks' provisions and roaming 20 miles from the nearest road, and then packing out a bull elk on your back, you're dreaming. The amount of food and gear needed for two weeks, particularly during cold weather, will weigh 80 to 90 pounds, and a bull elk will require about five trips at 100 pounds each. You had better invite Superman along on your hunt if you plan to tackle that chore.

Realistically you have to gear a backpack trip to your own strength and endurance. For me, backpacking has been ideal for hunting as far as three to five miles from the road for up to a week at a stretch. This kind of hunting allows me to hunt farther off-road than the average day hunter will venture, but the rigors of the trip don't destroy me physically. Before you set out on a backpacking adventure, do some packing at home to find out what you're made of, and then in planning your hunt, choose an area that's compatible with your abilities.

Hunting From Roads. Don't assume you must hunt wilderness to find elk. You may face more competition from other hunters near roads, but 75 percent or more of the elk hunting today exists in road-accessible areas, and you'll find plenty of elk there. Hunting in Oregon, I hiked 200 yards off a paved road next to a logging operation, and immediately walked into a herd of elk. Backup beepers on logging equipment were making so much noise nearby I scarcely could hear the herd bull bugling, but I still pulled him within bow range. In Arizona, a friend of mine said he used the noise of cars passing on a nearby highway to cover up his sounds as he stalked a bull. The point is, elk are where you find them, and that isn't always 20 miles beyond nowhere.

The car-camper actually has an advantage over backcountry hunters. In the wilderness, mobility is limited. With a drop camp, for example, you're tied to a central location, and in backpacking your range is limited by time and energy.

In contrast, by car you can travel roads freely to explore new areas, and you can radiate out much farther from camp than if you're stuck in a central wilderness camp. You also can drop buddies off at the top of a ridge to hunt down to a road below and use your vehicles in other ways to save yourself time and energy.

Hunting by road, you have several options. One is to stay in a motel. In some cases that will work, but realistically, most good elk country contains few motels, and hunting out of a motel will require an excessive amount of driving to and from the hunting area each day.

Some hunters tow camp trailers or small tent trailers into elk country. For early-season hunting, when roads generally are in good shape, that's a fine option, but a trailer does limit flexibility. You can't negotiate rough, backcountry roads with a large trailer, and even if you do, especially during October and November, you face the potential for getting stranded by heavy snow or rains.

You must have warmth and comfort to enjoy the rigors of an elk hunt, especially during the late season. A large base camp comprised of quality wall tents suits many hunters' needs.

A preferable option is to set up a large camp in a central location. Most serious elk hunters own several large canvas wall tents, each with a wood stove, and they erect elaborate tent towns for their annual elk trek. That's a practical arrangement for late-season hunting because it gives you a comfortable home where you can warm up and dry clothing after a cold, wet day in the field. A reliable, warm camp is essential for enjoyable elk hunting.

For early-season hunting—August and September—when shelter and warmth are not so critical, you can camp out of your truck, which allows you the greatest mobility. In many cases, successful elk hunting requires finding an area where undistubed animals have concentrated. Camping out of your truck, you can hunt an area one day, and if it doesn't pan out you can throw your gear into the vehicle and head to another spot immediately, and you can keep moving until you find an ideal location.

One commonly asked question is: How long should I plan to hunt? Finding elk can take time, and if this is your first hunt, you'll spend a few days just learning an area. I personally wouldn't plan for less than 10 days, and I feel more comfortable with two weeks.

Research

A personal contact may be your most valuable aid in planning a hunt. A person who knows the country and the animals can teach you more in one hour than you can learn in years on your own. If you don't have personal acquaintances in the West, contact game departments, forest service offices, sportsmen's clubs, or other groups to strike up a friendship. Even if no one can hunt with you, someone may take time to point you in the right direction when you arrive to hunt. The North American Hunting Club opens up many opportunities along this line, and chances are you can swap an elk hunt for an interesting trip in your local area.

Equally good would be to take a guided hunt your first time around. In the long run it could save you many dollars. One Minnesota hunter hired a guide his first year in Idaho, and then he returned on his own and killed elk the next two years. In contrast, I've talked to hunters who've tried on their own for several years and have never seen an elk. It's a lot cheaper to hire a guide one year to learn the ropes than to spend four or five frustrating, elkless years on your own.

If you can't find a personal contact and refuse to hire a guide, you'll have to plan your own hunt from the ground up. That may seem like a prodigious task, but if you passed the test at the first of this chapter, you've probably got what it takes. Just don't skimp on the research. Hunters who complain about a bad experience generally set out half-cocked; those who make it on their own, research and investigate extensively. The value of research can't be overemphasized. Selecting an area can take time, and you can expect to run up some phone and postage bills, but the time and expense will be worthwhile, because in most cases the quality of your hunt can be directly related to the extent of your research. Over the past dozen years, I've planned many hunts to new areas. A few have bombed, but consistently when I've done my homework the hunts have far exceeded my expectations.

Remember one thing about hunt planning—it's not an exact science. Below I've listed the general steps, but this is not an exact prescription for a guaranteed hunt. Your success depends a lot on your ingenuity. But by applying some of these guidelines, you can assemble a composite picture of conditions that should lead you to a good hunt.

Picking A State. Many hunters arbitrarily pick one state because a friend hunted there or they read about it in a magazine. I think that's a mistake, as one example points out. A fellow from Arkansas wrote and said he had problems hunting the San Juan Mountains of Colorado because he had heart trouble and the elevation there was too high. His doctor told him to hunt at lower elevation, and he wanted to know such a spot in Colorado. Apparently he assumed Colorado was the only state worth hunting for elk. In reply I told him to hunt elsewhere. The lowest point in Colorado is 3,800 feet, and in elk country the lowest elevations are closer to 7,000 feet. In most places you hunt from 9,000 to 11,000 feet. My advice was to hunt in Idaho, Montana, or Oregon where elk live in lower country.

Unless you have good reason to hunt one particular state, begin your research by ordering big game regulations for all Western elk states. (If you want to hunt on your own, forget about Alberta and British Columbia—unless you live there—because these provinces require nonresidents to hunt with guides). Studying all the regulations is the only way to get an overview, and you must know the range of possibilities before you can make a wise choice.

Some states, for example, offer six-week bow seasons and a month-long rifle season. Others have split seasons that fall in either October or November. Some states have seasons only in October, and others have seasons during the rut. Some states do not have rut-hunting seasons for rifle hunters, but they do for bowhunters. Check for restrictions on the number of hunters, and see whether the state offers limited-permit "trophy" areas or special antlerless licenses. And, of course, look at the license and tag fees. Also, if you want to plan a combination hunt, say for deer and elk, examine the regulations for this potential. In some states combination hunts are possible, and in others they're not.

When you send for regulations, ask for harvest statistics as well. Don't be misled by sheer numbers. For example, in Colorado the total elk kill is close to 30,000 and average hunter success is 17 percent. In Arizona the total kill is less than 2,000 elk, but rifle-hunting success ranges close to 35 percent, and the average bull is much larger than in Colorado. At the same time, read everything you can get your hands on about different states and regions. At the library, the *Readers Guide To Periodical Literature* lists hunting articles in outdoors magazines by state, so you can get some good ideas there.

Read books, too. Many of Jack O'Connor's writings take you on adventures in the West's famous elk regions. The Boone and Crockett and Pope and Young record books serve as definitive directories to trophy hunting. Reading also may give you further sources of information—people that you can talk to for more specific details.

Audio tapes, like these on bugling, and video tapes can be an important aid in planning your self-guided elk hunt.

In addition, utilize the wealth of taped material available these days. Dozens of companies produce video and audio cassette tapes, many of which take you right along on actual hunts, and some companies produce video movies of hunting. Tapes and movies are no substitute for first-hand knowledge, but they can give you a feel for the experience. A friend of mine bought a couple of tapes on elk bugling from Wilderness Sound Productions of Springfield, Oregon. He listened to the tapes over and over. By the time he went hunting he felt like a veteran elk hunter himself, and on his first hunt he enjoyed thrilling action from day one. Few tapes give you a concrete idea of where to hunt, but they can make you familiar with the overall elk hunting experience so you face fewer surprises when you start hunting.

Maps. Once you've settled on a state or two, order public land maps—in most cases these will be national forest maps—for the entire state. Also order state topographic maps from the U.S. Geological Survey. A map is little more than an aerial picture of the country, and while sitting in your living room, it provides you with a view of prospective hunting country. From maps you can determine the elevations involved, general topography, the nature of drainages, the road systems, accessibility, the proximity of towns, facilities, campgrounds and many other necessary aspects of a hunting trip. Eventually, different areas will begin to stand out in your mind. Note these areas and begin to make a list of questions, which will serve as the basis for further research.

Personal Contacts. Next to actual scouting, locals who know the territory and the conditions are your best sources for information. What you're looking for is experience, and lacking your own, the next best thing is somebody else's. Plan to contact hunters, biologists, foresters, and other sources by telephone. The person who won't spend five minutes writing a letter will talk for an hour on the phone.

A couple of general guidelines apply to all phone research. First, ask specific questions. If you simply call a person and say, "Can you tell me that best place to hunt in Colorado?" your answer will be something like, "Well, the whole state has good hunting." Then you're no better off than when you started. Besides, general questions promote vague answers. However, if you call up and ask something like "I've noticed that Bear Creek has no roads into it, and game department figures show good hunting success there. Can you tell me what the country looks like in Bear Creek, and why the hunting success is high there?" In response to a question like that, a person either must say, "I'm not telling," (and if he says that, the place is probably worth investigating further), or he has to give you a specific, useful answer. As you interview people over the phone, have a complete list of questions at hand, and keep maps of the areas discussed in front of you for quick reference.

The other reason to do some research ahead of time is to gain the confidence and trust of those that you are interviewing. Hunters call me frequently to get information. If a guy obviously has done no homework and is simply looking for a free lunch, I'm evasive. On the other hand, when somebody demonstrates that he has researched on his own and is on the right track, I find myself opening up, probably because I'm willing to help someone who has tried to help himself. Sometimes I even reveal secrets I should keep quiet.

Here's one final guideline: double-check your findings. Never take the word of just one source. I try to contact three sources on each prospective area. If one person tells me an area is excellent hunting for big bulls, I then call another source, and then another. If they all say, "Yeh, man, that place is full of big bulls," then chances are it's true. But if their responses contradict each other, I'm skeptical and dig further before committing myself.

Big game biologists may be the most valuable sources because they work with animals year around, and as public servants most are fairly free with their information. However, some biologists aren't hunters and they view game herds different from a hunter's point of view, so don't stop with biologists. From your reading try to get the names of hunters in the area. You can probably make contacts through sporting goods stores or writers for the local newspaper. Also contact forest service and BLM offices and talk to resource people there. They spend plenty of time in the field and often will share their observations.

Your line of questioning will vary, depending on your goals and your findings from previous research, but some topics apply to most hunt planning. Below I've listed topics I always try to address, and this list may help you scout by phone:

1) "Biology" Of The Area. This has to do with the quality and quantity of elk. If you simply want to kill an elk, regardless of size, look for areas with the highest elk densities. One clue is total harvest. Units with the highest harvest probably have the most elk. In parts of northeast Oregon, for example, big bulls are scarce, but elk are numerous and chances for killing a small bull or cow are excellent. The same applies to the famous White River country in Colorado. Elk densities are high so your chances of seeing animals are good, but because hunting pressure is high, few bulls live long enough there to reach trophy status.

If you simply want to kill a meat animal, consider applying for a tag in one of the many limited-permit antlerless hunts. Most states offer cow tags, and these tags are most commonly issued in areas with excessive numbers of animals.

To assess the number of animals in a given region, ask biologists how they would rate densities in certain drainages—low, medium, or high? Hunters or loggers probably won't think in terms of densities, so ask something like: How many elk could I expect to see in a day of hard hunting? How many herds of elk live in the Black Creek drainage? One? Five? Ten? If I hunt there during the rut, how many bulls could I reasonably expect to hear bugling during a day of hard hunting? Two? Fifteen?

If you want a trophy bull, say a mature 6-point or larger, the criteria differ. One starting point is the Boone and Crockett record book. It points out those areas where some of the largest bulls have been taken. From this you can discern which counties or national forests have produced trophy animals.

Another way to determine the trophy quality of an area is the bull-cow ratio. In high-production areas with a high elk harvest, the bull-cow ratio may be as low as 5-10 bulls per 100 cows. In other areas where hunters are limited for one reason or another, the bull-cow ratio may be as high as 30-40 bulls per 100 cows. The greater the percentage of mature bulls in the herd, the better your chances are for taking a trophy animal. Most authorities agree that the post-season ratio should be 20 per 100 or higher for good trophy hunting. In some cases, you can get figures that show bull-cow ratios, but it takes some digging. It's easier to ask local biologists: Which drainages have the highest bull-cow ratios? Why is that true?

In any good trophy area, hunting pressure is limited in some way. In many cases, it's a function of natural conditions. Inaccessibility may be one, and that's why the percentage of mature bulls generally is higher in deep wilderness than in well-roaded areas.

However, don't be fooled into thinking wilderness holds the only good bulls. In many cases true wilderness, such as the Bob Marshall in Montana or the Selway-Bitterroot in Idaho, gets hunted heavier than more accessible regions. That's because the general rifle season runs for two months in many wilderness areas, and outfitters hunt there intensively for the full two months. For that reason, fringe country with small roadless blocks scattered among accessible drainages often has better trophy potential than deep wilderness. Few outfitters operate in such country, and there's enough backcountry to provide good sanctuary for elk.

Terrain and vegetation may also serve as natural sanctuary for trophy bulls. In parts of northern Idaho and Montana, the jungle-like brush and trees provide elk with good refuge cover in well-roaded country, so trophy bulls survive even amid intense hunting pressure. In southwest Colorado, some rugged canyons will make you dizzy just looking up at them. If you've got the grit to hunt such places, you can find trophy bulls within a quarter-mile of paved highways. Ask local sources about the potential for such sanctuary areas. It seems like every region has its notorious "Hell Hole" or "Black Canyon" where nobody in his right mind would shoot an elk. If you're after a trophy, that's the place for you.

Finally, don't overlook man-imposed sanctuary. Many states restrict the number of hunters in certain units to promote quality hunting. Colorado has designated several units as "trophy areas"; Utah has some limited-entry hunts that produce huge bulls; all hunting in Arizona is limited entry; Oregon has "3-point or better" units that maintain high numbers of bulls. In most cases, limited-entry systems yield higher hunting success than general seasons, and the bulls generally are bigger. Inquire about the quality of limited-entry hunts.

2) Access. Along a similar vein, you want to determine access. Your maps show roads, but from that you can't necessarily determine the quality of the roads, especially under varied weather conditions, and you can't determine the current status. Logging, mining, and other development continually open up new roads, so all maps are necessarily out

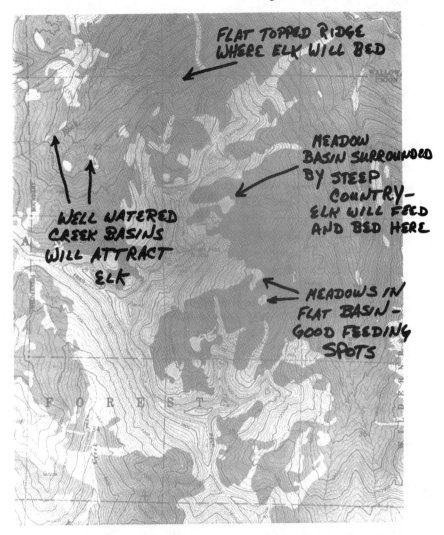

FLAT TOPPED RIDGE
WHERE ELK WILL BED

MEADOW
BASIN SURROUNDED
BY STEEP
COUNTRY-
ELK WILL FEED
AND BED HERE

WELL WATERED
CREEK BASINS
WILL ATTRACT
ELK

MEADOWS IN
FLAT BASIN-
GOOD FEEDING
SPOTS

GOOD PLACES TO FIND ELK

Topographical maps will be important to your initial selection of a hunting area and again later on when you begin actual scouting. Maps quickly reveal to the skilled eye where elk may be found.

of date even before you get them. Many states have imposed road-closure systems, some only during the hunting seasons and others permanently, so roads shown on your maps may not be open to travel. Also, many old maps show trails that in many cases no longer exist, and in other cases have been turned into jeep roads. During your research, ask about the present condition of the road systems and trails, and update your maps to avoid time-wasting surprises when you start hunting.

3) Terrain and Vegetation. Elk country varies infinitely. In the higher ranges of Colorado and Wyoming, you find "classic" elk country— timberline basins and alpine meadows, pockets of black timber, frigid springs bubbling from the ground. In parts of Colorado and Utah, however, elk thrive in nasty canyons with oakbrush and aspens. In northwest Montana, elk country consists of steep, low-elevation mountains blanketed with mile upon mile of endless timber. In Arizona and New Mexico, major herds thrive on pinion-juniper flats that look more suited to lizards. In other words, there is no such things as "typical" elk country. You want to start out with a valid picture in your mind, so ask local sources: What kinds of trees are these shown on my maps? Is there heavy underbrush, or is visibility good? Do tight contour lines shown on my maps represent cliffs, or simply steep hills? By asking such questions, you can gain a clear picture of the country.

4) Movement And Habits Of The Animals. In some regions, elk are primarily grazers, and in other regions, where meadows are scarce, they browse on leafy plants. Ask locals what the primary forage plants are, and at which elevations you can expect to find most elk. In some country, they'll stick to a narrow elevational band right at timberline, and in other places they're scattered throughout forested slopes.

Also, ask about movements and migration patterns. In some parts of the Southwest, elk live year round in one small locality. In mountainous, high-elevation country, they may move up and down considerable distances depending upon immediate conditions. An early frost can force animals from the high country down into the lower river drainages where the feed remains green. A heavy snow storm could push them from one drainage into another. During a wet year, they may congregate around certain meadows, but following a dry summer, when those meadows dry up, the elk may move into heavy timber or other well-watered areas to seek lush feed. Ask locals what elk would do under various conditions. That way, if you don't find animals in one kind of habitat or at one elevation, you'll know where to continue the search.

5) Livestock. Some areas are heavily grazed by sheep and cattle, and I've found it frustrating trying to hunt elk among herds of cattle and sprawling bands of sheep. Find out if livestock roam the same ranges

Be sure to check out the availability of water for your camp needs. In some places it's plentiful, in others you'll have to bring water in with you.

you plan to hunt, and if they'll be moved out by the time the hunting season opens.

6) Campsites And Water. In many areas, water is no problem because springs and creeks are numerous, but in other regions, water may be scarce and you may have to bring your own. In some places you can camp about anywhere, but in other regions camp spots are at a premium. Get some suggestions on prospective campsites before you set out.

7) Weather. Weather will influence your campgear and clothing selection. During August and September, you would expect warm, balmy weather, and you'll probably get some like that, but you're just as likely to get snow. Later in the season, you can expect blizzards and deep snow and temperatures down around zero. Always ask about the weather and determine what would be the worst type of weather you could anticipate and prepare accordingly.

Scouting

The final planning step, once you arrive at your prospective hunting area, is scouting. Before you start, it's important to understand the

A good topo map allows you to begin scouting your selected hunting area while sitting at your kitchen table.

When you first arrive in an area to hunt, getting an overview of the country is most important.

nature of elk. If you've hunted nothing but deer, you might have trouble adapting to elk and their unique habits. First, remember that elk are herd animals, and they'll range in small bands from two to three animals up to a dozen or more. Unlike deer, which may be scattered evenly throughout a mountain range, elk herds will live in specific pockets, and the territory between herds may be elkless.

Habitat To Look For. Elk are heavy bodied animals with very thick coats, so particularly during the early fall, you'll find them primarily on north and northeast slopes where temperatures are coolest and vegetation is thickest.

Elk hang out around wet meadows and spring seeps where moisture cools the air and where they can wallow in the mud. The heads of drainage basins and low points where springs ooze from the ground are good locations. Elk are primarily grazing animals, so any area that has lush, grassy meadows and parklands adjacent to heavy cover for bedding and refuge may attract elk. In some regions, grass feed is scarce, and there elk will feed on alder trees, huckleberries, and other leafy browse. As you scout you want to look for these cool haunts with good feed.

Topographic features often serve as a guide for locating elk. High alpine basins with grass on the higher slopes and heavy timber for bedding at the lower ends often attract animals. Most elk country is very steep, so animals frequently bed on small, flat benches.

Hunting pressure, especially during rifle seasons, can influence the location of elk. As you scout, try to pick out pockets of heavy vegetation or roadless drainages where the elk can find refuge from hunters.

Scouting Methods. Before you start hunting, it's essential to have an overview of your country. Try to arrive a couple of days before the season so you can look around before you start hunting. Even if you arrive during the season, you're smart to spend a couple of days looking before you even consider hunting. Unless you have a personal contact to show you where to camp and where to hunt, I suggest that you not set a permanent camp until you've scouted and have decided where to hunt.

One way to get a quick overview is to hire a local pilot to fly you over the country for an hour or two. An aerial view can save you many hours of scouting on the ground.

If that's not possible, pick out vantage points. Fire towers present the best views, but any high mountain, bluff, or ridge top that gives an overview is ideal. Drive to these points and simply look at the country. If you're on foot, it's not quite so easy, of course, but anytime I hike into new country to hunt, I first climb to the top of the highest ridges just to look around. It's time and energy well spent.

From any good vantage, use your binoculars to inspect the vegetation and terrain. You'll spot benches, basins, pockets of heavy timber, meadows, alder draws, north slopes and other features that might attract elk. And don't forget to look for elk themselves. If you watch at daybreak and dusk, chances are good you'll spot herds feeding in the open, and right there you've saved yourself many miles of walking.

Also in scouting, drive every road in the area, or hike and ride the trails. That might seem like a waste of gasoline or energy, but familiarity with the road and trail network will contribute immeasurably to your hunting efficiency.

One other thing as you're scouting—take time to chat with anyone you meet. One tip from a local could be make a trip. One year my friend Larry Jones was bowhunting when he met a man scouting for the rifle season. They struck up a conversation and the man mentioned where he'd seen a 7-point bull. Larry made a mental note, and the next day he drove to that location and found that very elk. He saved himself many hours of scouting by being friendly. Never pass up the opportunity to

When conditions change suddenly a good map and knowing how to use it will reveal the most likely hunting spots.

chat with other hunters, loggers, or foresters.

Maps. Another valuable scouting tool is maps. With topographic maps, an item you should never be caught without, you can do much of your scouting while sitting in camp. Look for basins, benches, north slopes, saddles, heavy pockets of timber, springs, heads of creeks, and other localities that would provide the feed, water, and cover desired by elk.

In many cases you can pinpoint the location of animals before you even look at the country. As an example, in Wyoming's Wind River Range, Roger Iveson and I sat by a warming fire one afternoon, lost in the fog. Visibility was less than 50 yards. This was our first time there so neither of us knew the area, and since we couldn't see our surroundings in the fog, we were basically lost.

"Let's look at the map," I suggested. "Maybe we can get some ideas from it." We found our location on the map right beside a river. Just across the river, on a north-facing slope, the map showed three small drainages. At the lower ends they were very steep, but higher they flat-

This hunter took his bull in the dense fog because he knew how to let his topo map help him find game.

tened into small bowls. They looked good for elk.

"Let's cross the river and hike into those basins," I suggested. "Unless you've got a better idea."

"We could sit by the fire," Roger laughed. "But then, we probably won't kill any elk here, so let's go."

In the dense fog we needed a compass to find our way up the steep ridge, but as the terrain flattened out we knew we had hit the first basin. We bugled there several times and got no response, so we hiked on to the second. We bugled and a bull responded instantly. To make a long story short, we called in the bull and Roger nailed him. In many cases, you can use maps in that way to discover likely elk haunts.

As you scout, note wind patterns, too. Wind may be the most significant influence on your hunting plans, because you can't fool an elk's nose. Within a given area the wind generally has definite patterns, so try to map these out as you learn the territory, and use this knowledge later as you plan day-to-day hunt strategies.

After a couple days of such scouting, you'll have an overview of the land and know specific localities that might hold elk. You can now set up camp in a central location and plan your hunt.

Reading Sign

One final step in scouting is reading sign. In most cases you'll simply combine this step with hunting, evaluating sign as you travel from one likely spot to the next.

Tracks and droppings are the most obvious sign. In general, elk tracks look like overgrown, blocky deer tracks. First try to determine the freshness. If the tracks are frost crumbled, you know they're at least a night old. If they've been rained in, they were made before the latest storm. If there's snow on the ground, you should be able to tell whether the tracks have been frosted or snowed in, or whether the wind has blown snow into the tracks. Press your fingers into the mud, snow, or dust to give yourself a "freshness" comparison.

A yearling cow's tracks are about three inches long, those of a cow or small bull 3½ inches long, and the tracks of a large bull are four inches or longer. Rounded tracks don't necessarily mean "bull." The front hooves on all elk are broader and more rounded that the hind hooves. I've measured several and have found that on large bulls, the front hooves are four inches long and four inches wide, and they're blocky almost like the hooves of a domestic cow. The hind hooves are also four inches long, but they're only 3½ inches wide and have the pointed appearance of deer hooves. The same general shape relationship holds for all elk. I measured the hooves on a yearling, for example, and the front hooves were three inches long and three inches wide; the back hooves were also three inches long, but they were only 2¾ inches wide.

During spring and summer, elk eat green grass and their droppings look like small cow pies. When the animals are feeding on browse—which generally is the case in the fall—their droppings are in the form of pellets. Usually they're about the size of olives, and a bull's pellets are dished on one end, like a pitted olive.

Fresh droppings are green and soft. In damp weather they might stay green for some time, but the inside will harden up. In dry weather, droppings will turn black quickly. If they're still moist inside, however, you know they've been made within the last day or two. If you find fresh tracks and droppings, rest assured that elk are nearby. Unless disturbed and run out of the country, an elk herd will stay in a small vicinity for a long period of time.

During the rut, you'll look for other sign, too. Rub trees are very common where bulls battled trees and shrubs. Don't ignore rubs, but don't put all your faith in them either, because the bull could have moved on. A rub doesn't mean much unless it's accompanied by fresh tracks and droppings.

Wallows where bulls have rolled in the mud also should catch your

This elk track is about 3½ inches long and three inches wide. Judging from the size and shape, it's probably the hind track of a cow. It is a couple days old.

eye. If the water in a wallow is still muddy, you know a bull has used it recently and he may still be nearby.

On Your Own

With mere words on paper, no one can teach you how and where to hunt elk. However, the ideas outlined here have served me well in planning more than a dozen self-guided elk hunts. Even with careful planning, your first hunt or two might prove frustrating, but on the other hand, you might start out like my friend Mike Gerber from Nevada.

Mike had hunted deer extensively, but he had no experience with elk. He bought a book on elk hunting and listened to several tapes, and he made a number of telephone calls to Colorado to get information on different areas.

He drove to northwest Colorado the day before the bow season opened and set up camp. Early opening morning he pulled on his camouflage clothes, painted his face, and hurried up the mountain toward a promising aspen park. He blew his bugle and got an immediate response. At first he felt sure it must be another hunter, but he wasn't positive, so he set up and bugled again. In a short while, a bull arrived on the scene and Mike brought him down with an arrow. He had hunted a good full hour!

I can't promise you that kind of success, but if you'll follow the guidelines above and persevere long enough to learn, I think you'll enjoy some fantastic elk hunting—on your own!

Planning A Self-Guided Hunt — Research Resources

The addresses here will get you started in planning. These are major offices for each state and region, and from these you can get the addresses and phone numbers for all lower offices.

State Wildlife Offices

From state wildlife agencies you can obtain current hunting regulations, information sources such as the names of biologists, maps of state-owned hunting lands, and in most cases, a list of guides and outfitters in that state. Elk hunting is very limited in Nevada and California, but for the sake of completeness addresses for these are listed as well as the major elk states and provinces.

Alaska
Department of Fish and Game
P.O. Box 3-2000
Juneau, AK 99802
(907) 465-4100

Arizona
Game and Fish Department
2222 W. Greenway Road
Phoenix, AZ 85023
(602) 942-3000

California
Department of Fish and Game
1416 9th Street
Sacramento, CA 95814
(916) 445-3531

Colorado
Division of Wildlife
6060 Broadway
Denver, CO 80216
(303) 297-1192

Idaho
Fish and Game Department
600 S. Walnut
P.O. Box 25
Boise, ID 83707
(208) 334-3700

Montana
Department of Fish and
    Wildlife
1420 East Sixth
Helena, MT 59620
(406) 444-2535

Nevada
Department of Wildlife
Box 10678
Reno, NV 89520
(702) 784-0500

New Mexico
Game and Fish Department
Villagra Building
Santa Fe, NM 87503
(505) 827-7899

Oregon
Department of Fish & Wildlife
P.O. Box 59
Portland, OR 97207
(503) 229-2403

Utah
State Department of Natural
    Resources
1596 W.N. Temple
Salt Lake City, UT 84116
(801) 538-4713

Washington
Department of Wildlife
600 Capitol Way N.
Olympia, WA 98501-1091
(206) 753-5700

Wyoming
Game and Fish Department
5400 Bishop Blvd.
Cheyenne, WY 82006
(307) 777-7735

Alberta
Department of Forestry, Lands
    and Wildlife
Main Floor, North Tower
Petroleum Plaza
9945-108 Street
Edmonton, AB T5K 2C-6
(403) 427-6733

British Columbia
Ministry of Environment,
    Wildlife Branch
780 Blanshard St.
Victoria, B.C. V8X 1X4
(604) 387-9717

U.S. Forest Service

From these central offices you can get a complete list of National Forests for each region. There is a nominal cost for these maps.

Region 1
(Montana, Northern Idaho,
  Western North Dakota)
Federal Building
Missoula, MT 59807
(406) 329-3316

Region 2
(Colorado, Kansas, Nebraska,
  S. Dakota, E. Wyoming)
P.O. Box 25127
Lakewood, CO 80225
(303) 236-9427

Region 3
(Arizona, New Mexico)
Federal Building
517 Gold Avenue S.W.
Albuquerque, NM 87102
(505) 842-3292

Region 4
(Nevada, Utah, Southern Idaho,
  Western Wyoming)
Federal Building
324 25th Street
Ogden, UT 84401
(801) 625-5605

Region 5
(California, Hawaii, Guam,
  Trust Territories)
630 Sansome Street
San Francisco, CA 94111
(415) 705-2870

Region 6
(Oregon, Washington)
P.O. Box 3623
Portland, OR 97208
(503) 326-3625

Bureau of Land Management

Ask for a free State Index Map. These list all BLM maps for each state. Prices vary but most maps cost about $2. For Index Maps, write to Bureau of Land Management, State Office at these addresses:

Arizona
P.O. Box 16563
Phoenix, AZ 85011
(602) 640-5504

California
Federal Building, Room E-2841
2800 Cottage Way
Sacramento, CA 95825
(916) 978-4746

Colorado
2850 Youngfield St.
Lakewood, CO 80215
(303) 239-3667

Idaho
3380 Americana Terr.
Boise, ID 83706
(208) 384-3016

Montana
P.O. Box 36800
Billings, MT 59107
(406) 255-2913

Nevada
850 Harvard Way
P.O. Box 12000
Reno, NV 89520
(702) 785-6586

New Mexico
Federal Building
P.O. Box 1449
Santa Fe, NM 87504
(505) 988-6316

Oregon and Washington
P.O. Box 2965
Portland, OR 97208
(503) 280-7287

Utah
University Club Building
136 S. Temple
Salt Lake City, UT 84111
(801) 524-5311

Wyoming
P.O. Box 1828
Cheyenne, WY 82003
(307) 775-6256

Topographic Maps
First ask for free state index maps, then from those order the specific state, regional, county or quadrangle topographic maps to cover your hunting areas.

Branch of Distribution
U.S. Geological Survey
Federal Center
Denver, CO 80225
(303) 236-7477

Books To Aid Your Planning
An invaluable source of information sources is the *Conservation Directory*. It lists addresses, phone numbers and the names of contacts in all state and provincial wildlife agencies; offices for federal land management agencies; private conservation groups throughout North America, and much more. This book is a must for anyone seriously planning a hunt. Contact:

National Wildlife Federation
1400 Sixteenth Street, N.W.
Washington, D.C. 20036
(202) 797-6800

The Wildlife Management Institute has published a book called *Elk Of North America, Ecology And Management.* This is a comprehensive treatise on elk. It doesn't tell much about hunting, per se, but it exhaustively explores the habits of elk and their habitats, and it serves as valuable background information for hunt planning. This book sells for $39.95. Check local bookstores or contact:

North American Hunting Club
P.O. Box 3401
Minnetonka, MN 55343

3

Booking A
Guided Elk Hunt

Two factors contribute greatly towards a sportsman's decision to book a guided elk hunt. First, he must greatly desire a successful elk hunt. Second, he must be able to afford to pay the price for it.

A hunter has the best chance of killing an elk on a guided hunt because he will have the services of a guide who knows the land, knows the elk, and knows how to find the bulls. In other words, a hunter books a guided hunt because he wants his elk hunt to be successful, and he is willing to pay to improve his chances of taking home a trophy.

The price of a guided elk hunt can run well over a thousand dollars. Some men save for years, pinching pennies by skipping lunch at work, so that they can one day take that dream hunt for the mighty bull elk. Other men, who can afford it, don't even think twice about laying down a couple thousand dollars for a guided elk hunt.

Just about all of us fall into one or the other of the above categories. It doesn't matter whether you saved for years for your elk hunt, or you simply wrote a check for it, the key to a successful guided elk hunt is to enjoy yourself. I have had both types of hunters in my camp—the poor and the rich—and certain individuals from both ends of the monetary ladder have displayed increasing dissatisfaction when the last day of their hunt arrived and they had not killed an elk.

A guided elk hunt should be an enjoyable experience for a hunter, and if you spend all of your time figuring out how much money you wasted with each succeeding fruitless day, you're not going to enjoy

***There's no doubt about it. The guided hunter has the best odds of bringing his
hunt to a successful conclusion.***

yourself. In fact, I tell clients to consider the money already spent and
gone when they book a hunt. I tell them to quit worrying about how
much money they spent, and to start looking forward to an exciting hunt
that only a few fortunate sportsmen ever get the privilege to experience.

The Decision To Hire An Outfitter

The decision to make a guided elk hunt quickly leads a sportsman
into that uncertain chore of finding the right outfitter. It is a little scary
hiring the services of a man whom you have never met, and it's even
more frightening to send a large down payment to a complete stranger
who lives hundreds or thousands of miles away. You need only mention
that you are planning to hire a guide, and you will immediately hear

horror stories about unscrupulous guides who have fleeced nonresidents. Fortunately, very few of these stories are accurate.

Every western state and Canadian province strictly controls the outfitting done there. Before a person can become a professional outfitter, he must first pass a competency test. A performance and insurance bond are also required before a license is issued. Not until all these requirements are met can a person advertise an outfitting service. In addition, records of each client must be submitted annually to the overseeing agency.

Choosing A State

The proper way to begin your search for an outfitter is to narrow your search down to a particular state. The previously mentioned western states and Canadian provinces in chapter two all have huntable elk herds. However, several other factors may make you lean towards a particular state. It may be that you want to hunt in those beautiful high country aspen groves in Colorado, or perhaps the heavy forests of western Montana appeal to you. Another factor is a state's proximity to your home. If a NAHC member from Texas has no special preference which state he hunts elk, he would be smart to pick a nearby state such as Colorado or New Mexico, rather than Montana.

A big factor contributing to a hunter's choice of which state to hunt is in the associated big game animals that may be encountered on his hunt. A few years ago a man from Minnesota contacted me about an elk hunt in Montana. He informed me that he was weighing my offer against that of another outfitter in a neighboring state. During the course of our conversation, he mentioned that he was a trophy whitetail hunter. I informed him that we had some huge whitetail bucks in my area, and they were not hunted enough to be overly spooky. The man was amazed! He thought that Montana had only elk and mule deer! Consequently, he booked with me, and I helped him kill the largest whitetail buck of his life. He also killed a dandy five-point bull elk on the last day of his hunt.

Choosing The Type Of Elk Hunt

The next matter for a prospective elk hunter to decide is which type of guided hunt to take. There are four basic types of hunts to choose from—bare bones, drop camp, standard hunt, and deluxe trophy hunt. There are pros and cons to each type of hunt, and a hunter must weigh such things as cost versus success potential when choosing the hunt for him.

Bare Bones. The bare bones hunt is the most inexpensive type of guided hunt. Usually, a client will be furnished room and board at an outfitter's main lodge or camp. The outfitter will recommend several nearby areas to hunt, but the client is left to hunt on his own.

This hunt is best suited for someone who wants to experience the thrill of elk hunting in the western wilderness, but wouldn't be overly disappointed if he went home empty-handed. Also, this type of hunt is better suited for a younger man who can travel up to five miles before the sun is up so that he can be back where the elk are found during the prime morning hunting hours.

The advantage of this type of hunt is its low cost. It is only a fraction of the cost of a standard guided hunt. However, expect to pay extra for packing out game.

The disadvantage is that a hunter's chances of success are very low. On a standard guided hunt you pay a guide mostly for his knowledge of the area, plus his expertise in finding the elk in a vast wilderness. Given the low price of a bare bones hunt you simply cannot expect this type of service.

Drop Camp. An outfitter will furnish several additional services to a client who contracts for a drop camp elk hunt. The outfitter will furnish a fully equipped backcountry camp, complete with tents, cooking utensils, and usually food. Transportation is furnished into the backcountry where the clients are dropped off at the camp. The outfitter leaves them to hunt on their own after pointing out areas to begin hunting. A guide will stop by every other day to tend to any needs the clients may have, plus pack out any game.

This is a good hunt for a group of men who already have some knowledge of elk and how to hunt them. However, it still does not furnish that critical ingredient to any successful contracted elk hunt—*guide expertise.* Even an experienced elk hunter will use up several days just locating the elk.

The main advantage of a drop camp hunt is its cost—about half that of a standard guided hunt. Also, a drop camp is usually far enough back from civilization that hunting pressure from other hunters is minimal. The client is in good elk habitat without a long walk every morning.

The con is that all cooking and camp chores must be done by the client. He must locate the elk on his own, and then plan a successful hunt. Also, a client must field dress, quarter, and hang any game killed. This is a massive chore even for an experienced hunter.

Standard Guided Hunts. The standard guided hunt is taken by most hunters who hire the services of an outfitter. With this type of hunt, the outfitter furnishes a guide, usually one guide for every two hunters. All packing, camp chores, and field care of game is taken care of by

Most elk are killed by clients on standard guided hunts where the guide provides about everything except the hunter's gun and sleeping bag.

the outfitter. A client need only bring his gun and sleeping bag for this type of hunt. Also, the hunter's knowledge of elk hunting need not be great, since he has a guide to find the elk and plan the stalks.

A hunter who is serious about killing an elk would be wise to consider this type of hunt. In fact, most elk are killed by clients on the standard guided hunt. That critical guide expertise is well worth the price when he gets you within range of an elk.

One big advantage of this type of hunt is the convenience of having everything furnished for you. Add to that the benefit of a guide, and you can see why most serious elk hunters choose the standard guided hunt.

The big disadvantage is the price, usually over a thousand dollars. Also, a client does not have his own personal guide at his disposal. If only one bull elk is seen within shooting range, it may not be your day to shoot if you are hunting with another client.

Deluxe Trophy Hunt. The deluxe trophy elk hunt is for a sportsman who has a specific requirement regarding the minimum size bull he will kill. Usually, most trophy elk hunters want to kill at least a six-point

This six-point bull would be about minimum requirement for most trophy hunters.

bull. And I've even had clients give me a trophy measurement that they want their bull to score. Recently, a man told me he did not want a bull smaller than 330 Boone & Crockett points.

This may seem a bit overbearing, but I believe that it is a good idea because often times a bull might have six points on each antler, but its antler size will be smaller than most five-points. Most experienced hunting guides can guess within a dozen points what a bull will score even at long range.

Heed one note of caution. A client should be fully aware that a deluxe guided trophy hunt is often more physically demanding and sometimes even less exciting than the standard guided hunt. One client that I had for a deluxe trophy hunt became increasingly disgruntled because the other clients who were on a less expensive standard elk hunt were seeing many more elk than he was, and they were working much less to do it. I explained to him that the big, trophy-sized bulls were staying far back in remote areas away from the cows and younger bulls, and that it would take some tough hunts into these backcountry hideouts to find his trophy. Unfortunately, he did not find his trophy bull, and he left camp feeling that he had been short changed.

The pro of this type of hunt is the privilege of having a personal guide at your disposal. Also, every outfitter has a few remote areas set aside where he knows the big bulls tend to hide out, and he'll save those areas for his higher paying clients who are after a specific trophy-sized bull.

The con is that a client may actually pay much more for this type of hunt, but have to work much harder to kill his bull. Also, less game may be seen because the hunting is done far back from where most of the elk herd lives. Sometimes, a client may hunt for ten days and not see another animal other than the trophy bull he kills.

Choosing An Outfitter

Every outdoor magazine contains several pages full of outfitting advertisements. Each ad sounds exciting, and many sportsmen are prone to contact and hire the first outfitter whose ad catches their eye.

This is a poor, risky way to book a guided hunt. It's not that there are a bunch of dishonest outfitters out there—it's just that each client has certain requirements for his hunt, and not every outfitter is capable of furnishing the type of hunt desired.

At least a half dozen outfitters should be contacted and these should be carefully weighed against each other concerning such things as hunting success, accommodations, the hunting area, the price, etc. Questions should be asked—lots of them—until you know exactly what to expect from each outfitter. Misunderstandings between clients and out-fitters about things that were not fully discussed can sour a hunt.

Booking An Archery Hunt. Outfitters in recent years have awak-ened to the potential of guiding bowhunters. The outfitter who had only six weeks of guiding rifle hunters each fall now also books a month of archery hunts. Unfortunately, guiding a bowhunter for elk requires special techniques which the average outfitter does not possess. It's not enough to know where the elk are in an area, a guide must also understand the requirements of the bowhunter. He must be aware that his job is to get his client within 30 yards of an elk before the archer has a chance for a kill. Most guides simply do not have that expertise, and for that reason, I would suggest that any bowhunter planning a guided elk hunt should lay down some stiff qualifications for an outfitter.

First, and most important, the outfitter should be an experienced elk bowhunter himself. Only a guy who is experienced in the unique needs and limitations of an archer can efficiently lead his client on a guided bowhunt for elk. And even better than that, he should have been a successful elk bowhunter. Then at least you'll know he has an under-standing of the great sport of bowhunting elk. Second, it might be ac-ceptable to book with a nonbowhunting outfitter if he has guided other bowhunters who were successful. Some guides catch on to the tricks of bowhunting after a while and eventually become good bowhunting guides.

You may have to contact several outfitters before you hit one who seems to have some working knowledge of guiding bowhunters, but unless you book with a proven outfitter, your guided bowhunt may end up a confusing ordeal in which the guide doesn't know any more than the client.

Success Rates And References. Some outfitters advertise success rates that are extremely high. One ad I read recently for deer and elk rifle hunts claimed a success rate of 80 percent. I knew for a fact that this outfitter had not had that good a season, so I asked the man about his success rate.

In reality, only 15 percent of his hunting clients killed elk, but there were many young mule deer bucks in the foothills of his hunting area, and almost every hunter managed to kill one before his hunt was over. Did this outfitter lie? He doesn't think so, but his ad could mislead a client into thinking that he has an 80 percent chance to kill an elk if he books with this outfitter.

Another instance of misrepresenting success rates occurred when an outfitter put an ad in a magazine with sparkling descriptions of his hunting area and the enormous herd of elk that lived there. He claimed

A good bowhunting guide must know how to cope with the self imposed limitations that the archery hunter faces.

75 percent five- and six-point bulls, leading anyone who read his ad to think that 75 percent of this outfitter's clients killed five- or six-point bulls. In reality, the outfitter meant that of all the elk that were killed, 75 percent of those were five- and six-point bulls—the rest were cows or spikes. His overall success rate was much lower.

When you ask an outfitter about his success, be specific. For instance, ask him how many elk hunting clients he had last year and how many elk were killed. That way you can figure out the success rate yourself, and the possibility of being misled will not occur. Generally, I've found that a 25 percent success rate for rifle hunting clients is a decent rate. With bowhunters, it's about 10 percent due to the difficulty of getting close to an elk.

However, a low success rate can be deceiving. I know a few outfitters with low success rates who hunt in areas where mostly mature bulls are taken. A high percentage of six-point bulls killed annually by an outfitter may be more attractive to some clients, even though the overall success rate is low.

Every prospective client who contacts an outfitter wants references. However, phoning someone in reference to a hunt really doesn't tell you anything about that outfitter. Even the worst outfitter is going to get lucky once in a while and one of his clients will kill an elk. And naturally, the lucky client will say nice things about the outfitter.

You might be wise when asking for references to request the names of two clients from the previous year who were *not* successful. If they were given a good hunt, and the guide tried hard to find an elk for them, that's as good a recommendation as the guy who killed an elk.

NAHC Hunting Reports

North American Hunting Club members are truly fortunate to have the *Keeping Track* newsletter section in *North American Hunter* magazine which deals with hunting reports on outfitters that club members have hired to guide them. This section gives the name and address of the outfitter, and the club member gives his rating on such things as accommodations, game populations, and hunting success.

This is an excellent place to start your search for the outfitter who is right for you. Pick a few outfitters who sound interesting and start digging for information, and remember to get all the names of NAHC members that a particular outfitter has guided, whether or not they were successful. Contact these members for an honest appraisal.

Likewise, the North American Hunting Club's listing of Approved Guides & Outfitters is a good publication for selecting a guide/outfitter. It lists the names and addresses of all outfits in U.S. and Canada

Success rates can be deceiving. An outfitter with a low success ratio may be attractive to a trophy hunter because of the large number of six-point or better bulls taken by his clients.

which have been approved by the majority of NAHC members hunting with them. Specific reports are available by contacting the NAHC.

Initial Contacts

The best way to initiate contact with an outfitter is by mail. Write a letter explaining the type of hunt that you are interested in, and request information on his outfitting service which should include a price list.

It would be smart to write at least a half dozen outfitters in order to compare hunting areas, success rates, and prices.

Immediately after you have received some outfitter's info, you will realize whether or not his type of hunt is for you and you will be able to narrow down your selection.

The next step is to phone the outfitter that interests you most. This is a vital part of selecting the right outfitter because it will give you some feel for the man's personality. If he doesn't talk much over the phone, and his answers are all "yes" or "no," he probably isn't going to do much more talking during your guided hunt. Work your way down the list of acceptable guiding services, asking questions, but mainly getting the feel of the man on the other end of the line.

You should have a list of specific questions which have arisen while you read over an outfitter's pamphlet. During your phone conversation, make these questions to-the-point, and expect a specific answer in return. Below is a list of questions you should ask any outfitter. You may have additional specific questions about your planned hunt. And don't be afraid to phone an outfitter several times while you are still searching for the right one, especially if additional bothersome questions arise.

Questions To Ask An Outfitter:
1) What type of terrain is the hunting done in? (Is it steep and brushy, or gentle open parks, etc.)

2) How is his operation run? (Determine if he seems too disorganized.)

3) How many hunters does he handle annually and on a weekly basis? (A large influx of clients each week may mean that you will not receive the best in personal service, though some large outfitting services still manage quality hunts for clients.)

4) How many hunters per guide? (The standard is two hunters per guide.)

5) Ask for North American Hunting Club references, if possible.

6) Will there be any additional expenses? (Transportation to and from the airport, packaging and shipping meat, etc.)

7) What additional game can be hunted in case an elk is killed early in the hunt? (Ask about special hunt permits in the area, such as sheep, goats, moose, etc.)

8) What is the success rate for elk hunters? (Be specific so that the outfitter understands your desire for a true picture of your chances of making a successful elk hunt.)

9) Ask the outfitter his opinion on the best time during the season to book a hunt. (Find out if those time slots have been filled yet.)

10) What price variations can be made to accommodate the type of hunt you are interested in? (This is the time when you should detail the type hunt you want—drop camp, trophy hunt, etc.)

Prices vary greatly, and that is why you should get price lists from several guiding services. There is no state-controlled standard for charges to clients, and this is an area where the client is on his own. He must be the final judge whether or not an outfitter wants too much money for his services.

Unfortunately, it's not as simple as comparing the price for a known commodity, such as new car. The quality of service varies among outfitters, and so does the price. I know one outfitter who felt that he could not furnish clients with quality hunts if he herded them through his camp like so many cattle. Consequently, he now takes only two hunters at a time, but be charges more than most of his competitors. But clients get a first rate hunt, and his success rate is higher than other outfitters.

Your conversations with references will help you assess whether the outfitter is charging too much for what he puts out. Find out from these hunters if camp was comfortable, and if the guides worked hard to find game. Ask if they were satisfied with the price that they paid, whether or not they killed an elk.

Most bookings are done unofficially over the phone. A client eventually narrows his choices down to that one outfitter who can furnish the right kind of hunt. During this phone conversation, you should inform the outfitter that you want to book a hunt. Go over the time slots open with him and decide on the dates that you want your hunt to take place, and then tell him that a check will be in the mail tomorrow.

It is vital that the outfitter be aware that you want a definite booking slot over the phone. I once had a prospective client who phoned me several times, and while he sounded interested, he never asked for booking dates or sent a down payment. Imagine my surprise three months later when I received his down payment check in the mail. Unfortunately, I was already booked for his required time slot.

The day after you have agreed over the phone to book with an outfitter, send a certified check via registered mail. Request that the outfitter send you in writing his acknowledgement of your down payment, plus your hunting dates. Otherwise, both you and the outfitter may be chagrined to discover that the dates you thought you had were not reserved due to human error during the phone conversation many months earlier.

Your booking may be for a hunt two years in advance, but keep in touch with your outfitter during the off-season each winter preceding your hunt. You will get to know him better, and you'll also be kept current on how his latest clients have fared. Be sure to phone your outfitter a month before your planned hunt and discuss your mode of transportation to his hunting area. It would be wise to phone once more a couple days before your hunt begins to give him your plane's flight number and arrival time so that he can pick you up if you are flying. If you drive, you'll have to agree on a place to meet.

Minimum Standards

Every hunter must decide what his minimum standard will be before he kills an elk. Some hunters will kill the first legal elk that they see, while others try to hold out for a bull. The trophy hunter has a high expectation and sticks to it. I've seen all of these types of hunters, and I appreciate every one of them. They made their own decision on what

In the waning hours of an expensive 10-day hunt, this raghorn might become a trophy for most any hunter.

kind of elk they would kill, and they stuck with it.

I've also watched a man quickly change his mind when the opportunity to kill a lesser elk suddenly presented itself. I once had a trophy hunter change his mind and shoot a four-point bull on the day before his hunt ended. The man in this instance did some quick soul-searching and realized that his chances of killing a big six-point bull on the last day of his ten-day hunt were slim, and he went home pleased with his bull.

I allow a client to set his own standards, but when a hunter asks my opinion on the matter, I counsel him on what I call progressive elk hunting. I suggest that a first-time elk hunter should not set his trophy sights too high. First, he should kill a bull elk, and then he can go after a trophy bull on his next hunt. I also suggest that he might hold off shooting a cow or spike bull the first couple days of his hunt while we are trying to find him a large bull, but as the hunt nears an end, a cow or a spike can indeed become a fine trophy elk to take back home.

What To Expect From An Outfitter

An outfitter should furnish all the services that he and his client agreed on when a hunt was booked. In addition, an outfitter should try hard to get his client a killing shot at an elk. After the hunt is over, the outfitter should bring both the client and his trophy out safely and see to it that the client is on his way back home on the agreed upon date. That's the simple, general description of an outfitter's duty.

Now to specifics. The most critical service that the outfitter performs for a client is guiding. You should be furnished with a competent guide who knows where to find the elk, how to hunt them, and what to do with such a huge beast after it is killed.

The problem in this situation often arises after a bone-weary client has hunted hard for several days without even seeing an elk. He suspects that his guide is inept, or that the area he is hunting in does not have any elk. Sometimes there is a good foundation for a client's suspicions about his guide. Often, an outfitter will be stretched so thin with his guides that he will occasionally hire someone who is not a good guide.

But any client should fully understand that the reason an elk is a top trophy animal is because it is very difficult to find, hunt, and kill in the vast expanse of Western wilderness. Elk do not have the convenient daily patterns that prove fatal to deer. An elk may be on a particular sidehill one morning, but be five miles away the next. It may take your guide a few days to find the elk and figure out the best way to hunt them. Have patience, and don't become discouraged because you haven't seen an elk during the first couple days of your hunt.

You should also expect a full day's hunt every day that you have booked with an outfitter. Sometimes, a guide will suggest that you take an afternoon off if he feels that you could use some extra rest after a particularly strenuous hunt. That is a decision that *you* should make, not him! But first weigh his plans for the upcoming day. If it is a strenuous hunt with an excellent possibility of killing an elk, you may be wise to rest up for it.

Bowhunters should be aware that elk hunting in the early fall is best in early morning and late evening. It is a waste of time to stomp around in the heat of the day when the bulls have quit bugling and are bedded down in thick cover. The sensible thing to do is to retire to camp when your guide suggests it.

You should also expect accommodations in camp to be adequate. Food should be in good supply, and comfortable cots furnished. But remember, a backcountry camp will not have all the comforts of home such as a flush toilet or shower, and a spike camp will have even less.

An outfitter also has the responsibility to help a client get his trophy back home in good condition. That may mean making arrangements to have the meat cut up and frozen, then packed in sturdy cardboard boxes for the long trip home. Also, antler tips should be covered with cardboard and taped to protect them and other baggage during transportation. Airlines require it!

What An Outfitter Expects From A Client

An outfitter expects his client to be in reasonably good shape. I tell all my clients that their chances of success with elk are directly proportional to their physical conditioning. If a guy can't hike a half mile without resting, then he's going to miss the elk when a strenuous hike is necessary to catch a feeding herd before it enters the timber.

A client who is out of shape will wear out quickly. After three days of hiking over rugged terrain, a man who is 30 pounds overweight is usually so stiff and sore that only a short hunt can be planned for him. And forget about the "easy" way of getting around in the mountains; a horseback ride for a guy who is 30 pounds overweight will leave him just as stiff and sore as if he had walked.

An outfitter also expects his client to be able to shoot straight. This is an area where many clients fall short. A guide who gets his hunter a 300-yard shot at a bull elk has done his job. If the client misses that shot, he has failed in his job. Many sportsmen are used to short range deer hunting, and the prospect of taking a 400-yard shot seems ridiculous. Today's high powered rifles are made to deliver a killing shot at ranges up to 400 yards, and any client who has an elk hunt booked would be wise to do some long range target practice.

Camp Manners. Foul language and abusive alcohol consumption will not be tolerated in an outfitter's camp. The cook may be the outfitter's wife or another female. Foul language in her presence will usually lead to a sticky situation where the outfitter must order the client to either stop swearing or stop talking.

Some outfitters have their own brand of justice for a boozer. They feel that any guy who gets drunk at night deserves to be hunted hard the next day. I usually inform a heavy drinker that it's his money to waste, but he should not expect to kill a bull elk if he wakes up with a hangover every morning.

Last, but not least, is a client's attitude toward the hired help. The camp help is not answerable to a client, only to the outfitter. Any complaints about them should be issued in that direction. A client who continually complains about his guide will lessen his chances for success during the hunt. A guide who feels appreciated will be sure to work hard to live up to a client's opinion of him.

Tipping Your Guide. A guide receives little more than minimum wage for the strenuous work he performs, and it is customary for a client to show his appreciation toward his guide by giving him a tip at the end of the hunt. Tipping is not done only when an elk is killed. A client should tip his guide if he feels the man tried his best throughout the hunt to find an elk for his client. In addition, a tip should be given to a guide if his expertise helped the client kill an elk.

How big should your tip be? Some clients lavish their guides with hundreds of dollars. But, I believe, the average tip should be about $50 for a guide who has worked hard for his client, plus an extra $50 if an elk was killed. Since tipping is a personal gesture, if you do tip, give what you feel comfortable giving.

If the sound of a bull tearing apart the brush with his antlers doesn't get your adrenalin flowing, nothing will.

4

Hunting The Rut

If you're new to elk hunting, you might first ask: What's the big deal about bugling? Why is hunting the rut any different from any other elk hunting?

Weather. Traditional elk hunting in October and November calls for snow and ice-box temperatures that demand heavy clothes and a major camp set up. In contrast, you often can hunt in your shirt sleeves during the rut, which takes place in September. Granted you can get some nasty weather during that time—it's been rare that I haven't seen at least one good snowstorm in September—but usually temperatures are tolerable and you can camp and dress fairly light. In many areas the trees are just taking on their autumn colors and the first frosts are whitening grassy meadows at night, and it's a pleasant season to spend in the woods.

Elk Availability. Elk also are easier to find during the rut. By nature elk are obscure animals that spend the better part of their lives in dark timber, out of sight of man, and they sneak around with aggravating stealth. To find them, you must rely strictly on your eyes, and to some extent your nose—elk are fairly strong smelling. To say the least, non-rutting elk are difficult to locate. During the rut, in contrast, they bugle and that's your ace in the hole. In my opinion, the toughest part of elk hunting is locating animals, and the option of locating them by sound gives you an immeasurable advantage.

Calling. In addition, you can call them in. If you've perfected duck or predator calling, you know the value of calling, and the same advantage is yours in calling elk. Rather than trying to stalk a bull on his terms, you take a stand and call him to you on your terms.

The fact that you can call-in elk establishes rut hunting as the ideal time to hunt trophy bulls. Because you can locate elk more easily than at other times of year, chances are you'll have opportunity to look at more bulls. In addition, bulls lose some of their innate caution during the rut, and you'll have an easier time getting a look at the biggest bulls.

Finally, the rut adds an emotional dimension absent from conventional elk hunting. The sound of a whistling bull stirs up the blood of most hunters. The idea of hunting a raging beast on a reckless rampage adds an element of excitement and involvement you'll never experience when the woods are silent and the elk are skulking around.

Bowhunting offers the most widespread opportunity for bugling because all western states with major elk herds have archery seasons in September. However, in some cases special muzzleloader seasons fall during the rut, and in the backcountry of Wyoming, Montana, Idaho, as well as British Columbia and Alberta, general rifle seasons take place during the rut. Wherever you hunt elk, bugling for bulls will prove to be unique and unforgettable.

When Should You Hunt?

One of the most commonly asked questions is: When should I hunt—early in the rut or during the peak? Rut timing will vary slightly by region, but generally speaking the rut begins at the end of August and lasts through early October. From late August through September 10, bulls are roaming to find cows and activity is pretty loose-knit during this period. The so-called peak of the rut lasts roughly from September 10 through the end of September, and during this time most bulls will spend their time hanging around centralized herds of cows. By early October, many of the cows have been bred and the animals start drifting off into smaller herd units again, although you may hear bulls bugling through mid-October.

Many hunters misconceive that the peak of the rut promises the only good action. The last two weeks in September is good, no question about it, but in my opinion, the earlier in the rut you hunt, the better. I've hunted from late August through early October, and consistently my best success at bugling-in bulls has been early in the rut. That's not to say I've heard more bulls then, only that I've called more in. Frequently these early bulls bugle little if at all. They often come in silently, but the fact is, they come to a call eagerly.

Terry Lonner, an elk biologist in Montana, agreed that early bulls are easier to bugle in. He said that early in the rut, bulls are very active

One advantage to hunting the rut is the pleasant weather you can expect during September throughout the West.

as they roam to look for cows, and their anxiety level is high. As a result, they're less wary than later when they've settled into established breeding herds. I also figure they've been harassed less by hunters early in the season, so they're probably less spooky and call-shy than later.

During the peak of the rut in later September, bulls have pretty well established a hierarchy centered around a nucleus of cows. The bulls have been rutting hard and are wearing down, and the same bulls have been bugling at each other day after day. When a strange intruder enters the picture, the bulls may be cautious about taking up his challenge. You may hear a lot more bugling during the peak of the rut, and the bulls often go wild, but overall I have found them tougher to call into close range at this time than early in September.

Some hunters may avoid hunting the early rut because of a myth concerning rut timing. Many times I've heard hunters say they couldn't find any bugling bulls because hot weather delayed the rut. That simply isn't true. Weather in the fall has nothing to do with timing of the rut; the urge to breed is triggered by what biologists call the "photo period." Put simply, the length of daylight at a given time each fall triggers a hormonal change in the animals, and that change occurs at the same time each year, regardless of the weather. During a hot, dry fall, elk may spend most of the day in cool, dark timber and breed primarily at night, but rest assured, come early September, they're in rut whether or not you hear them bugling.

Hunters also frequently ask about moon phase. They feel they should time their hunt to coincide with a dark moon because, they assume, elk will be more active during daylight hours then. Again, that's a myth. The fact is, elk don't need moonlight to see at night. I've heard them bugling throughout nights that were so dark I couldn't see my hand at arm's length. The darkness didn't seem to slow them down much. On the flip side, I've enjoyed some excellent bugling throughout the day following bright moonlit nights.

Again Terry Lonner's studies support these observations, During the 1970s, Lonner followed radio-collared elk for up to 50 hours straight, day and night. Lonner said activity level at night seemed to be about the same, regardless of moon phase. In short, don't fret the moon.

Learning To Bugle

Some people think bugling is a way for bulls to attract cows, and others say it's a way for one bull to intimidate or challenge other bulls. In reality, bugling probably serves these functions as well as others we'll never understand. To keep things simple, I'll just say elk communicate by bugling, and they bugle most heavily during the breeding season. As far as hunters are concerned, the purpose of bugling is irrelevant. The fact is, bulls do bugle, which helps you to locate them, and they do come to a call, which helps you to get a shot.

The Kinds Of Sounds. Before getting into bugling methods, let's look at some various sounds. Bugling and the associated grunting noises of a bull in rut are the sounds most commonly associated with elk hunting. The "average" bugle starts on a low note, rises for several octaves, holds a high whistling note for two or three seconds, and then descends back through the scale. At a distance most bulls sound like a flute or calliope, but that can vary greatly. Some bulls sound like they're screaming in pain, some resemble moaning hereford bulls, and others sound like they're gargling Listerine. It's hard to say exactly what a bull sounds like.

In addition to the bugle sound, bulls grunt and chirp and chuckle. It's impossible to describe all of this on paper. You must either hear bulls in the field (or in the local park), or you can buy tape recordings of bulls. Several companies produce excellent elk-bugling tapes. To learn bugling, listen to all of the sounds on these tapes, and practice until you can duplicate them.

Rutting bulls also make a lot of general racket as they rub their antlers on trees and thrash brush in mock battles. These sounds can play a part in calling a bull. I generally term this aspect of calling "raking on a tree." To produce antler sounds, you simply get a stick two or three inches in diameter and rub it on a tree trunk and thrash limbs with it. You want to sound like a bull that's mad at the world and has decided to tear it apart.

A third sound that's effective in hunting elk can be termed cow and calf talk. My friend Larry Jones, a student of elk hunting, has recorded herd talk on a number of occasions, and he has taught me a lot about this aspect of calling. Primarily the mewing and chirping sounds seem to be a communication among cows and calves. From a distance you might think you're hearing a flock of gray jays. The use of mewing sounds can be significant in hunting elk.

Choosing the Sounds. How do you know what sounds to make? Bugling for elk can be broken into two steps: locating a bull, and bugling him in. For locating a bull, you primarily use the bugling sound. The high pitched note carries a long distance, and often when a bull hears that he'll respond by bugling.

At closer range, however, you may need a repertoire of sounds to pull him into shooting range. You can still bugle, of course, and in some cases a couple of well-timed bugles are all that's needed to bring a bull on the run.

That may raise a question in your mind: What should your bugling sound like? Many elk hunters say they can distinguish big bulls from small bulls by the sounds of their bugling, and they further say the idea is to sound like a squeaky little bull because no bull in his right mind will come to fight a big bull that might whip him.

In my opinion, that's all hogwash, primarily because I doubt that any hunter consistently can tell the size of a bull by the sound of his voice. Hunting in Montana, Larry Jones and I heard a bugle so effeminate we scarcely took it seriously. "That's a little raghorn," we agreed. Pretty soon the bull walked into view, and to our astonishment it was a whopping 6-point. On the other hand, I've called in bulls that raged and bellowed lound enough to scare off King Kong, and as often as not, these have been little more than average-sized animals.

Dean Krakel II, in researching his book *Season Of The Elk*, observed and recorded dozens of bulls, and he said in his book that size and age have no bearing on the sound of bugling. Also, I talked to Terry Lonner about this. He said he can distinguish a spike bull from an older bull by its bugling, but among mature bulls—older than four years—he doubts that voice is a reliable distinguishing feature. The average mature 5-point can scream and grunt just as loud as any Boone and Crockett 7-point.

Here's the point: Don't try to sound like a little bull or a big bull

When you can't figure out what to say to a bull, mimic him! That's what Dwight Schuh did to this big bull in Wyoming. The results are obvious.

or whatever. Simply develop a variety of elk-like bugling sounds, some high pitched, others gruff and growly. Some bulls respond better to one type of bugling, and others respond better to another. Try one, and if that doesn't work, try another.

As you work a bull, you may feel like a high-school sophomore on your first date and not know what to say. If that happens, simply mimic the bull. That might not work on a girl, but it will on an elk. In Wyoming I had come to a standoff with a 6-point bull and couldn't figure out what to do, so I mimicked him. Every time he bugled, I bugled identically. When he grunted and squealed, I grunted and squealed. When he screamed with rage, I screamed with rage. Pretty soon he got so mad he marched down the hill to whip my tail, and I laced him with an arrow.

If you can't pull in a bull by bugling, just try grunting and chuck-ling. If that doesn't work, quit calling altogether and rake on a tree and thrash some brush.

At the same time, try some herd talk. A bull often will come run-ning to a supposed herd of cows when he'll stay away from another bull. In Montana, Larry Jones and I had followed a herd of elk some distance, and they quit responding to our bugling. However, every time Larry mewed like a cow, one of the bulls went hog wild. On that same trip we pulled in a small 6-point three times, even after he had seen us, strictly by mewing.

Making The Sounds. In recent years, elk calling, like everything else in the space age, has advanced rapidly, and many new calling devices have appeared on the market. Perhaps the most revolutionary has been the diaphragm call. This call was designed for turkey hunting, but it works just as well for elk, and it's the most versatile call available. With a diaphragm you can make any manner of squeals, grunts and chuckles, and you can make the mewing sounds of cows and calves. Further, the call fits in your mouth so you can blow it with no hand movement. That's a major advantage, especially for a bowhunter who must pull a bull in very close while keeping movement to a minimum.

Diaphragms do have shortcomings. They're fragile and eventually will wear out, so you want to carry some spares. Also, for some people they're hard to blow. If you have a high palate or missing teeth, you may have trouble using a mouth diaphragm.

The secret is to curve the tape on the call so it forms an air-tight seal against the roof of your mouth. Then, from way down in your stomach, you blow air across the latex diaphragm. With no tongue pressure, that should produce a low humming note. To raise the pitch, you increase tongue pressure against the diaphragm and increase air pressure. Several commercial tape recordings give detailed instructions on how to use a diaphragm. Most hunters blow diaphragm calls through a "grunt tube" to produce greater resonance.

Another diaphragm call is The Imitator. It has a latex diaphragm stretched over the end of a plastic tube, and you regulate the pitch by pressing your lip against the diaphragm. It's easier to use than a mouth diaphragm and it produces a range of realistic sounds. The biggest drawback is the fragility of the diaphragm.

The easiest-to-use and most durable call is the Larry D. Jones elk call, which has a stainless steel reed housed in a solid plastic head, and this is attached to a flexible grunt tube. With a quick twist, you can detach the reed head and use the grunt tube for bugling with your voice or a mouth diaphragm. To make this call work you simply blow; it requires

With practice, the mouth diaphragm allows the hunter to create an infinite array of elk sounds.

virtually no practice, and it's almost indestructible. This call makes an excellent bugling sound, and you can make mewing sounds with it, but you can't fine tune your grunting and chuckling with this call as you can with a diaphragm.

Voice bugling may be the best way to produce elky sounds, but many hunters can't do it. Children and women have high-enough voices that they can bugle, in essence, by screaming, but most men's voice are too low. Most voice buglers expel all the air from their lungs and then suck in forcefully to create a whistling sound in the throat. With some practice you may get the hang of this, and it's an excellent way to sound like an elk if you can do it.

Again, regardless of your bugling method, the only way to learn elk sounds is to listen to them. I'd suggest you buy three or four tapes from different companies and practice until you've perfected the sounds on those tapes.

Locating A Bull

As I've said, locating a bull may be the hardest part of elk hunting. These animals live in distinct herds, and herds may be widely separated by miles of empty country. For that reason, physical conditioning plays a big part in locating elk. If you're hunting by horseback or simply bugling off roads—which can work at times, although I feel a lot more confident bugling far from the nearest road—you may not need to be in great shape, but if you're hunting on foot, you must be prepared to hike 5 to 10 miles a day or more.

The general idea is to hike rapidly from one likely spot to another, bugling as you go. Often when bulls hear your call, they'll answer, and

To locate elk, hike through the woods, bugling as you go. Cover some ground and don't worry about making noise.

suddenly you've got a bull located. More or less. At least you know there's one out there somewhere.

From scouting and map study you should have a good idea of the likely spots, so try to plan your day's hunting to take you through several good locations. When moving from one spot to another, try to cover the ground as fast as possible. Sneaking around with the idea that you might walk up on a bull at any time only wastes time, because in bugling you're not looking for elk as much as listening for them. Unless you hit fresh sign, a good looking meadow area, or a bench where you feel confident elk could be bedded, move fast and bugle every quarter mile or so.

When you do come to a hot-looking spot or find fresh tracks, wallows, and droppings, then slow down and work it out carefully. By that I mean bugle often and give bulls plenty of time to respond. Bulls don't always answer your call instantly. They may hear you bugling, but they may do nothing for awhile, or they may only rake on a tree. Bugle three or four times over a period of 10 minutes and sit down and wait. Listen not only for bugling, but for other noises as well.

I located one bull by the sounds of his antler raking. I had bugled three times from the top of a ridge and had gotten no answer. Then below, at the bottom of a canyon, I heard some clattering, and each time I bugled, the clattering would intensify. Eventually I saw the bull and he was really tearing into a tree, but he never did bugle.

On another occasion, Larry Jones and I were hurrying through the woods, bugling as we went. We stopped momentarily to rest when I heard footsteps. "Larry, an elk is walking right toward us," I whispered. Larry looked at me crosseyed, as if to imply I were nuts, but I could hear the faint crunch, crunch of hooves.

"Really, listen!" I insisted. "He's walking right at us. Get ready!"

Larry drew an arrow and got set to shoot just as the tines of an enormous 6-point rack showed over a mound about 10 yards from us. The bull took about three more steps, oblivious to our presence, and Larry thumped him with an arrow.

On still another occasion, I had bugled several times and gotten no response when I heard a faint snap of a twig. Almost like a ghost a bull appeared 10 yards away, peeking at me over some low Christmas trees. The point is that bulls don't always repsond with violent bugling, so keep your ears and eyes open.

That leads to a few other points about locating elk. For one thing, always be ready. Even if you don't think there's an elk within 10 miles, if you blow the call, be ready. Hide in some brush and be watching, and never bugle from an open hillside where you could be seen. One

Keep moving until you hit fresh sign such as this wallow, then work carefully by bugling frequently and listening closely.

time a friend and I had hiked up a grassy slope and were sitting in the open when my friend impulsively blasted on his call. Instantly a bull screamed back right below us, and we couldn't move because we were in direct view of the elk.

You also should bugle fairly often to locate a bull, and that's true for a couple of reasons. One, if you wait to hear a bull before you bugle, you may never hear one. You have a call for one reason—to elicit a response from a bull. You don't wait for the elk to create the action. You create it by bugling.

Two, if you bugle infrequently, you could walk by a bull and never know he was there, or you could walk into a bull and spook him.

In Oregon, for example, I walked about 100 yards from my friend Pat Miller and bugled a half-dozen times over a period of 20 minutes. Getting no response, I returned to Pat's location.

"Man, you really got him going!" Pat said.

"What?" I said. "I didn't hear anything."

"You didn't? He answered every time," Pat said.

Standing there with Pat, I bugled again and sure enough, the bull answered right back. He was apparently down in a little pocket that muffled his noise. In broken country where sound doesn't travel well, bugle every time you come to a new draw or basin. You want to make sure you hear a bull before you unknowingly walk into him.

When To Bugle. One common question among newcomers to elk hunting is: When is the best time to bugle?

I see two different forms of bugling for elk. Some hunters are able to scout extensively and know their territory well, and they locate one big bull they want to hunt. In this case, the best times to bugle are early and late in the day when the elk are moving naturally on their own. You're only going to get so many chances at that one bull, and you want to go after him when conditions are perfect, because the more you spook him, the tougher he'll be to fool.

More commonly, hunters like you and me travel hundreds of miles to our hunting areas. We have little time to scout, and we're unable to pattern the movements of one specific bull, so we're pretty much hunting pot luck. In this case, I think you should bugle all day long to locate a bull. Except on extremely hot days, I've had just as much success locating animals at mid-day as early and late. Cool, overcast, drizzly, or foggy days are especially good, because animals may be active all day long.

However, I think the hunt-them-anytime philosophy deserves some qualification. On extremely windy days, your chances of locating a bull are very poor. In the Wind River Range of Wyoming, the wind blew

Cool days with a heavy overcast or fog are ideal for bugling because the animals will remain active throughout the day.

*Before you move toward a bull,
check the wind. You must be downwind or you'll never get close.*

unmercifully for three days. Roger Iveson and I bugled our heads off
during that time, and we didn't hear one bull. As soon as the wind let
off the fourth day, we got into elk. If you need a day of rest, take it
when the wind is howling through the trees, because your chances of
finding elk then are poor anyway.

Also in regard to wind, I suggest you back off when a storm is coming
and the wind is swirling. You can't fool an elk's sense of smell, and
chances are nearly 100 percent a bull will smell you before you can get
a shot if the wind is blowing all directions. For example, the wind was
whipping all over one day, but Larry Jones and I got impatient and decided
we'd chance it. After an hour of hiking and bugling, we finally got an
answer. At that moment the wind was blowing uphill, but then it shifted
down, and soon we saw the bull walking away deliberately, and he never
bugled again. He had smelled us, and we needlessly educated a bull.

You'll enjoy your best bugling where elk are totally undisturbed.
If you persist in hunting when wind carries your scent into every nook
and cranny, you'll eventually pollute the entire area with man smell. At
the worst it could drive elk out of the territory, and at the least it will
make them jittery and somewhat difficult to bugle in. Sitting in camp,
waiting for the wind to straighten out might not be your idea of fun,
but it's smart elk hunting.

Bugling In A Bull

In some cases, as you're covering ground to locate a bull, you might find yourself right in the hip pocket of an elk before you know it. That's why I say you should always be ready. At the first toot of your call you could find yourself face to face with a charging bull.

More often, however, you'll hear a bull in the distance, say from a quarter to a half-mile away, and rarely will an elk come to you from that distance. You'll have to get closer.

Before making a move, analyze the terrain between you and the elk, and determine wind direction. It's been said over and over, but the fact remains: you must have the wind in your favor. If the wind is blowing from the bull to you, then go straight at him, but if it's not, circle until you're at least cross wind, and better yet straight downwind of the bull. It doesn't matter whether you're uphill, downhill or sidehill from the bull. Just get the wind in your favor.

Then move toward him cautiously. I don't worry a whole lot about noise because elk themselves make all kinds of racket as they move about, but I definitely muffle man noises. Talking, coughing, nose blowing and whatever must be eliminated, and you should be wearing soft wool or knit clothes that slide silently past branches. Your nylon day pack should be covered with wool to prevent zinging off twigs and branches.

The sounds of your walking or breaking an occasional branch won't spook a bull, but there is a good reason for being quiet until you're ready to shoot—he could hear you walking and, thinking you're a bull, come on the run before you're ready. A couple of times I've been sneaking around to locate a good calling blind, and have had bulls come right in, even before I started bugling. I'm sure it was because they could hear me walking around.

As you're moving toward a bull, quit calling to avoid pulling the bull in before you're ready, although if the animal is a long way off, you may have to bugle occasionally to keep track of his location. Try to get within 200 yards or so before you set up to call him in. Most bulls will come eagerly over that distance. If you're not sure exactly where the bull is, be conservative and set up farther out. Often they're closer than you think, and you can always move closer later.

The Setup. My greatest elk-hunting frustrations have come from calling in bulls and then failing to get shots. In rifle hunting you have a little more leeway because of the nature of your weapon, but in bowhunting getting a shot is more critical. You must have a good setup.

That's especially true in brush country. In parts of Montana and Idaho, I've called bulls within 10 yards and less, and have been unable to shoot. In Oregon one year, outdoor writer John Higley and I hunted together for three days. In that time, we pulled three bulls within 25 yards of John, and he was unable to shoot at any one of them because of obstructions.

In some country, finding the ideal setup can be close to impossible, no matter how diligently you look, but in most cases bad setups are the result of haste. A good setup has several components, and foremost is shooting lanes. If you can't get a clear shot, there's no sense in calling in a bull, so look for a small meadow or a spot where distinct trails cut through the brush. You want to be able to shoot out to ranges of at least 20 to 30 yards.

At the same time, look for a place to hide. Ideally you need a tree trunk, dense Christmas trees, or stump behind you so you're not silhouetted. Avoid getting behind heavy cover that will restrict your ability to shoot. Sometimes I stand behind a small tree, but I cut out branches at eye level to form shooting lanes in all directions. If you're well camouflaged—and I believe in camouflaged clothing, face, and hands for bowhunters—you don't need heavy cover in front to keep from being seen. My friend Larry Jones always hooks a tree branch in his bow quiver to screen his face, and that helps hide you from a close-range bull.

Most important is to avoid movement. To help along this line, rest the lower limb of your bow in your pocket so the bow is held at eye level. For a longer recurve bow, you can sew a little pocket above the knee on your pant leg. With this support you don't have to strain to hold up the bow, and when you're ready to shoot, you can draw with virtually no movement except your drawing arm.

In looking for a blind, try to find a place that would hide an elk. When John Higley and I hunted together, we had a bull coming in before we were ready, so we picked blinds hurriedly. The bull was on one side of a draw and we were on the other, and the elk could see all of our side clearly. The bull came into view and then stopped to look around. John and I were well hidden and I'm sure the bull didn't see us, but he didn't see another bull either, and eventually he got suspicious and drifted away. Set up in such a way that you're not isolated out in the open where an incoming animal would be able to see another elk.

As you're looking for a blind, don't bugle. Just be as quiet as possible. In most cases you have plenty of time, and carefully selecting your setup with good shooting lanes and good cover will pay off.

Calling In Close. Now start bugling. In the average calling sequence, I bugle loudly and follow it up with some grunting and squealing, and then I rake on a tree with a limb. The bull normally answers back, and then I scream right back at him, as if he has insulted me. Some hunters are very tentative about bugling, and they call only in response to the

This hunter uses a branch in his bow quiver to screen himself from the elk when he draws. Notice also he is standing in front of a dense background to avoid being silhouetted.

Dwight Schuh doesn't wait for elk to bugle. He calls first and gets them mad! Note the bottom limb resting in his pocket. The bow is supported in shooting position without tiring his arm.

bull's bugling, but I've had better luck pulling in bulls when I've been the aggressor. The idea is to make a bull mad so that he'll lose all caution and charge in to take up your challenge.

Let me cite an episode in Montana that illustrates the classic bugling encounter. Mind you, it doesn't always work this perfectly, but this hunt involved most of the steps that you'll face in day-to-day elk bugling.

The time was mid-afternoon on a cold, overcast day. I had hiked to the top of a ridge overlooking a deep canyon, and I systematically walked out many finger ridges to bugle into adjacent draws. From three to six p.m. I got no responses and was beginning to think the elk had all pulled out, even though I had found some huge wallows and fresh tracks right on top of the ridge.

Just about the time I considered heading back to camp, I came to the head of a small draw to call one last time. Right below me, no more than 100 yards away, a bull erupted with defiant squealing and snorting, and the clattering of his antlers on a tree echoed through the woods. Here again, his presence took me off guard because I had been bugling regularly and yet hadn't heard this animal until we were very close together.

I thought about setting up right there and calling him in, but the

The results of Dwight's strategies. He released on this massive bull at eight yards.

wind was drifting across the hill from my left to right, and I figured the bull would come up to my right and smell me. So as silently as possible, I circled above the bull along a trail through dense huckleberries. He might have heard me slipping along, because he bugled fiercely a couple of times and was really tearing up some brush. The urge to bugle back was strong, but I wanted to get into the right position first.

When I reached a downwind position, I stepped into a grove of spruce trees and snapped off several limbs to assure a clear view. The mountain ash and huckleberry bushes were so thick, there was no such thing as an opening, but just in front of my blind the bush thinned for about 10 yards, and that seemed about the best I could do in that situation.

With an arrow nocked and my bow supported at eye level, I produced an angry, growling bugling with a mouth diaphragm call. The bull bellowed back instantly. I grabbed a stick and raked on a tree and bugled even more violently, and then I stood quietly to listen to determine what the bull was doing. Branches were snapping below me and I could see the tops of mountain ash bushes swaying as if a hard wind had come up. Then the ivory tips of antlers began to appear above the brush. The bull was coming and no further calling was needed.

For 30 yards the bull plowed through brush like Godzilla on the prowl, but not until he was 10 yards away could I see his body. I started to draw as he walked below me. Then he stopped and looked around. I froze. Rather than continuing below the blind he turned and came uphill to my left. I finished drawing slowly, and as he passed through a shooting lane eight yards away, I released the arrow. The bull whirled and mowed a swath through the forest for 75 yards. Then he crashed to a final halt. I was elated at taking a fine 6-point.

Dealing With Problem Bulls

That's the way it's supposed to work, and it does often enough to make us hunters feel real smart. But just as frequently, it doesn't, and then we find out we're not so smart after all.

The Herd Bull. Sometimes after you set up and start bugling, the bull will just take off running the other way. That's most common with a herd bull with cows. He's got his women, and he would rather keep them by running than by fighting.

If a herd bull runs, you have a couple of options. If you're in good shape, you can pursue the animals. They probably won't go more than a mile or so, and if you can keep up with them, you can try again. If you get in close enough and continue to harass the bull, he may very well get tired of your bothering him and come charging to challenge you. I know of several hunters who have killed bulls this way.

Possibly a better option is trying to stalk him. Herd bulls often bugle constantly as a display of dominance, so you can keep track of their location. Or if you have a partner, one of you can hang back and call to keep the bull bugling as the other quietly stalks in. If the herd moves away in a straight line and you're fast enough to circle ahead, you may be able to get in front of the herd to ambush them. So much of this depends on terrain and vegetation it's impossible to prescribe an exact formula for outsmarting a running herd bull. These are only some possibilities and I've made each work on occasion. You have to analyze each situation and determine which approach will work best under immediate conditions.

The Moving Elk. If you study a particular herd of elk enough, you'll probably detect specific daily movement patterns, and you can hunt them most effectively by ambush. In Arizona the animals make daily movements from water to feeding areas to bedding areas, and some hunters learn these patterns and use them to their advantage.

In Montana, Larry Jones and I hunted two different herds that appeared to have distinct patterns. When we first found them we simply moved in and started bugling. In one herd we could hear at least five bulls—probably a herd bull with cows and four perimeter bulls. Three times we set up fairly close to the animals, and three times they simply drifted away from us. They didn't run. They were just moving the other way. Later we talked to a local hunter who was familiar with that herd. He showed us a salt lick toward which the animals were moving, and he said the elk made a regular migration back and forth from that lick to a jungle-like bedding area. If Larry and I had known that to begin with we wouldn't have followed the herd. We would have got in front of them—between the elk and the lick—and ambushed them as they came towards us.

If a herd drifts away from you like that, they're probably not spooked. They're simply moving in a regular daily pattern. Rather than chasing along trying to bugle one off the back of the herd, you'll do better to circle in front quietly and bugle as they come toward you.

The Silent Bull. Often a bull will bugle vociferously at a distance, but when you get in close he'll clam up, or at least he'll refuse to come to you. Some bulls, like the one I killed in Montana, are hot and come on the run, but more often than not a bull will be cautious, and you may have to work two or three hours to get him in. Remember he lives out there and screams back and forth at other bulls all the time, so this is no big deal to him, and he's in no hurry to go anywhere. To get most bulls, you have to be more patient than they are.

If a bull continues to answer your call but won't come in after a

If a bull answers but won't come any closer, trying going to him. Slip in quietly and remain alert; ready to shoot. He might be sneaking up on you at the same time.

half-hour or so, try moving in closer to him. It seems that the closer you get, the more likely a bull is to come to you. You have to move very cautiously, because he could be sneaking around, looking for you.

Also, try different sounds until you hit a responsive cord. Dean Krakel II in *The Season Of The Elk* said he recorded many bulls and then played these recordings back to bulls in the field. Often when bulls heard the recordings they paid scant attention until a certain sound came along. Then they went wild.

That's why it's important to learn different sounds. Start out with a standard bugling sequence as I've described above. If that doesn't pull in the bull you're working on, quit bugling and just chuckle and grunt once in awhile as you rake and clatter on a tree.

If that doesn't work, quit making vocal sounds altogether and try quiet raking. I once watched a bull only 15 yards away as he raked a tree. He didn't clatter at all but simply peeled off small strips of bark with his brow tines, which produced a quiet scraping sound. He would do that for a half-minute or so, and then stop and listen intently and nibble the bark he had peeled off. Sometimes this kind of quiet activity will raise a bull's curiosity to the point that he'll come in just to see what's going on.

If bugling or raking won't work, try making some cow and calf sounds, as if you're a herd of elk just looking for some good-looking bull to come along. Often the mewing of a cow will stir up a bull when loud bugling only shuts him up. In many cases I mix bugling, raking, and mewing to create an overall "herd environment" sound that will put a bull at ease and hopefully will pull him in to see if he can get a cut of the action.

Again, there's no set formula that works in every situation. Through experience you'll get a feel for various situations, and you'll learn to make the right moves.

Getting The Shot

For a rifle hunter, bugling technique and the setup don't need fine tuning as they do for the bowhunter. Even at that, however, I think rifle hunters should take care to pick a location with good visibility that promises a clear shot. A sloppy setup just results in missed opportunities, or worse yet, in wounded animals that aren't recovered.

For a bowhunter, the only acceptable shot on an elk is at the lung and heart area. Getting that kind of shot may take patience. Often a bull will come in straight at you, and you must wait for him to turn to present a broadside shot. If you stand motionless and wait him out, you'll usually get the opportunity.

If a bull is walking broadside, stop him before you shoot. One time a bull walked downhill toward me. I drew my bow when the elk was 40 yards away and traced his movement until he passed an opening directly in front of me at 20 yards. The shot looked like a cinch, but my arrow hit a small fir tree halfway between me and the bull, glanced up, and bounded off the bull's back just above the pelvis. With my bow moving as I aimed, I was unable to anticipate every object in the way. For that reason, if a bull is walking I suggest you mew or grunt to stop him before you release. That way you can see any obstructions before you shoot.

How close should he be? Most elk hunting takes place in heavy timber, so shots generally are close range. Shooting ability varies with individual bowhunters, of course, and only you can judge how far away you should shoot at an elk. However, with patience you can pull most bulls very close, and I would say there's little excuse for shooting at a bull much farther than 30 yards away. In dense country most shots will be at ranges of 10 to 20 yards.

When you get a bull in like that, the only thing left is to heed my friend Larry Jones's favorite saying: "Pick a spot and shoot to kill."

5

Elk Hunting
After The Rut

Most sportsmen try to relate elk hunting to the deer hunting experience that they have gained in their home state. Unfortunately, there is a world of difference between the two sports. The land is different, hunting methods are different, and also the habits of the two species differ.

The deer hunter begins hunting immediately after he leaves his vehicle because the deer will be somewhere in the near vicinity, and his hunting technique is very slow and cautious. In contrast, the elk hunter cannot be sure that there is an elk within two miles of his position in the vast expanse of western wilderness. Consequently, he covers longer distances in search of an elk, and he moves at a greater speed through the forest.

The nonresident hunter who wants to kill an elk must radically change his long established hunting methods. This is a frightening prospect to the person who has spent his entire sporting life perfecting those keen hunting senses necessary for success when deer hunting. He must learn to hunt an entirely new way, and he usually has only a two-week hunting trip to do it. Fortunately, the elk can be somewhat predictable, and there is a definite method used by successful elk hunters. And the good news is that the average nonresident can become a successful elk hunter without an outfitter if he understands the differences between deer and elk hunting, and is willing to adapt his methods to western hunting.

How To Hunt Elk After The Rut, Before Snow

Most rifle seasons for elk begin after the rut when the bulls have stopped bugling. When the rut ends, the elk become nothing more than giant deer. In any drainage, they have certain tendencies concerning feeding, bedding, and movement and every knowledgeable elk hunter begins looking for elk by finding the answer to each of the above tendencies.

The most important item in the daily life of an elk is food. That is where the hunter begins his search for elk in any drainage. He must find out where such a huge animal finds the 20 pounds of feed it needs to sustain itself.

Certainly, it is not in the timber. Elk have many uses for the seclusion of the timber, but feed is not one of them. Trees exclude plant growth underneath, and while there may be some grass and brush to nibble on underneath the canopy of trees, elk need a much more concentrated food source. Find that food source, and you'll find the elk.

Elk feed in large openings such as the brush-choked sidehills in Idaho, the high country meadows in Colorado, or in the overgrown logging areas of western Montana. The serious elk hunter doesn't waste his hunting time wandering aimlessly through the heavy forest hoping to find an elk—instead he begins immediately searching these openings for elk.

If elk hunting was as simple as that, everyone would kill a big bull on their first hunt. Two variable conditions enter the picture which confuse and often discourage a new elk hunter. The fact of the matter is that elk are not found everywhere in a particular drainage, and their feeding patterns may be such that they are not in those openings feeding during daylight hunting hours. The obvious solutions to the above complications are to find the openings where the elk are feeding and then find out where the elk are staying when they are not in those openings. And once you understand how to do it, you will know the general "secret" of hunting elk.

The "Secret" Revealed!

The reason that most nonresident elk hunters fail is because they spend too much time hunting elk and not enough time scouting. A guy with only seven days to fulfill his dream hunt feels pressured to spend every available hour hunting elk. But if the elk are not right in front of him, he could easily spend all seven days hunting hard, but never see an elk.

You must do extensive scouting in order to find and kill an elk. I don't mean that a man from Georgia should take a midnight flight two weeks before his planned hunting trip so that he can scout for elk.

When the rut is on the wane and the season is moving toward real winter, elk will begin to make more use of dense cover areas. (Leonard Lee Rue III photo)

Scouting is done while the hunting trip is in progress. The correct way for a typical party of three hunters to begin their hunt is to spread out in a drainage and begin searching the openings for the few spots where the elk are feeding.

A hundred square miles sounds like an enormous expanse of land, but it is only an area 10 miles by 10 miles. Three men who covered several miles each day, carefully glassing the opposite sidehills of the drainage for elk, could cover such an area in a few days. Sooner or later, a herd of elk will be located, and then serious hunting can begin.

Scouting should be done from an elevation high up on a sidehill or on a ridge where the hunter has an excellent view of the large areas on the opposite sidehill. Actually, the elk could be on your side of the drainage, and you may spend a day or two glassing the opposite side, only to discover them after you have moved to the far side of the drainage to glass back where you just came from.

Look for the obvious feeding areas in natural openings or logging units. An area that looks perfect for elk, but doesn't hold any when you glass it, may be worth an extra look the next day. Also, glass sparse timber stands or small openings near suspected feeding areas. Often times, the elk will already have fed and are in the security of cover, and you will be able to spot them bedded down or milling around on their way to their bedding areas.

Glassing should be done with binoculars—good ones. I use a pair of Bushnell Custom Compact seven power binoculars that fit in my shirt pocket. Don't plan on using your rifle scope for scouting. After a few looks through the scope, your arms will grow weary and you will begin passing up many good sidehills because you don't see anything across that half mile expanse with your naked eye. At that distance, a dozen bulls could be bedded down in the open and you wouldn't notice them unless you used binoculars.

Elk are erratic in their movements. You may see them feeding in an opening an hour after dawn when you first spot them across a draw, but the next morning when you sneak in there expecting to find them, they are nowhere in sight. When this happens, it means that they began feeding at night, and you must decide where the elk go after they leave the feeding openings.

If the opening is near a ridge, expect the elk to be bedded down on the ridge. Elk like to bed on a ridge because they can see well below them and on both sides. If the opening is not near a ridge, expect to find the elk bedded above the opening. When there are two openings with a patch of timber between them, elk often bed down there, especially if the timber is thick.

Scouting is the "secret" that experienced elk hunters utilize to achieve success.

Get above an area where you think there may be elk, then glass down on them.

It is not unusual to spot a herd of elk feeding in an opening, but not locate them the first day or two. This is because elk have their own reasons for choosing where they will bed down. A herd may bed down only a hundred yards above an opening, or it may move a half-mile uphill to bed down on a ridge. This is when you must carefully move through the area, watching for tracks, and eventually you will narrow their bedding area down to the spot where the entire herd spends their days. A hunt can then be planned, and the result is usually successful.

If at all possible, move in on an elk from the same elevation on the sidehill or from above. That can sometimes be a problem. It seems that the elk are always above you, but if you move in on them from below, they usually see you first and escape. For that reason, you may have to take a circle route that gets you even with, or above, the elk. The hunter who moves down slowly and quietly from above on a herd of elk can expect to get the drop on them every time.

Now a word about the wind. Rifle hunting for elk usually means shooting at ranges in excess of a hundred yards, and at that distance, the elk rarely catch a human scent. Sure you should pay attention to it, but don't move in on an elk herd from an exposed side where they are sure to see your approach just to keep the wind in your face.

Standard Hunting Techniques—Still Hunting

The elk in some areas will be more widely distributed. There will be no large herds, but single animals and small groups will be encountered frequently. In this situation, still hunting works well. However, you should move about three times faster than you would if you were hunting whitetails. Elk are not as wary as deer, and you will be able to cover much more ground in a day of hunting.

The elk is a large animal, and is sometimes easier to see in the woods. But the old proven standard of searching for "parts" of the animal still is the best way to spot an elk. Look for the dark neck or tan rump of an elk. Also, the antlers of a bull will stand out. I've often studied a branch that just didn't look right, and then it turned into an antler when the bull moved his head.

You may encounter heavy brush or a thicket of timber while still hunting. There is no need to enter these areas and waste a lot of time if you can be certain that there are no elk in there. Circle the area and look for fresh tracks entering the thicket. The large hoof prints of an elk are easy to see and follow even on bare ground. If no fresh tracks are found, keep going.

Good binoculars, whether full-sized or compact, are crucial in successful elk hunting with any technique.

Hunting Techniques—Drives

A modified elk drive can be valuable, especially when you are reasonably sure that the elk are holed up in a particular brushy sidehill or area of thick timber. If there is an opening on the other side of the thicket, place a hunter or two there and then send a few hunters through the thicket.

When no opening lies on the other side of the timber, modify your drive by having everyone move through the thicket spaced evenly. The elk may see or hear the first hunter in front of them, and their tendency will be to move uphill and away from the danger. The other hunters will then have a chance to kill a fleeing elk.

The large size of an elk aids the hunter during these drives. A herd of elk running in front of a hunter will be heard even though they are 200 yards away. Often times during a drive, the elk spook and the hunter will hear the animals running out in front of him. The hunter should then charge forward and intercept the elk before they disappear. Don't sneak forward! Charge forward! A man running through the woods, at times sounds like an elk, and the other elk can think it's just another one of the herd moving towards them.

Hunting Techniques—Stands

A stand can be an effective aid for the elk hunter under certain circumstances. In the evening, some hunters take a stand overlooking an opening and catch the elk moving out of the timber to feed before dark. Another good place for a stand is along a well-used game trail in morning or evening. A tree stand works well in this situation because the hunter will be able to see better and the elk will not notice him high up in a tree.

Archery Hunting After Rut, Before Snow

Several elk archery seasons extend past the rut. Elk can still be killed at this time if an archer knows where to look for the elk and how to hunt them. Archers hunt elk wallows, game trails, and feeding areas after the rut with success. The only variation in hunting procedure from rifle hunting will be the need to get much closer for a killing bow shot.

Bull elk stop rutting, but they don't stop being vocal overnight. I've heard particular bulls emit an occasional bugle or grunt for weeks after the actual rut has ceased. In other words, the bulls aren't crazy with rut, but they will let their presence be known. And the archer who can pinpoint a bull's location because of an occasional grunt has a good chance to slip in on the animal.

Elk create wallows for relief from biting insects. They roll in the mud and plaster it on their hides for protection. Obviously, an elk doesn't have to worry about insects in October, but by then any wallow will have become a smelly meeting place for the animals. They will continue to come in to nearby wallows to drink and sniff the lingering aromas, and this is one of the best places for an archer to look for an elk.

Every creek has a few elk wallows where muddy shoreline or backwater exists. When you find an elk wallow, use a tree stand or wait downwind for elk in the evening or morning. Make sure your stand gives you a close shot at incoming trails and the wallow, but not so close that the elk spot you.

Trail hunting is another good archery hunting method for elk after the rut. You can use a tree stand or still hunt along a well used game trail for best results. It helps if you can spot a herd of feeding elk and then find the trail that they are using to move from feeding grounds to bedding area.

Elk Hunting In Snow

Snow works miracles for elk hunting. The odds tip heavily towards the hunter when the ground turns white. The elk are easier to see, they can be tracked in the snow, and as the snow builds up the elk habitat shrinks considerably.

Snow hunting also provides more trophy bulls. Those wise old monarchs grudgingly leave their backcountry hideouts when deep snow arrives. In fact, up to 80 percent of a drainage may be eliminated due to deep snow in November. The elk are then more concentrated, easier to see and find, and consequently easier to kill.

The elk can remain an elusive target for a hunter even with the benefit of snow. However, there is a wealth of snow hunting tips to push the odds even further in the hunter's favor. Some are small things to be noticed during the hunt, but when they are all taken into account, they usually spell the difference between success and failure.

Tracking. It's not as easy as it sounds. When the snow is two feet deep, you want to be sure that the tracks you are following belong to a bull. If you follow the wrong tracks and finally encounter a cow after an exhausting three mile struggle, you will be too tired to cut another track and keep going. It is vital that a hunter begins the day following the correct animal track, and there are ways to tell the difference between a bull and a cow print.

A bull's hoof is much larger than that of a cow. If a bull is traveling with a cow, you will notice the big difference in size, and also in the depth that the heavier animal pushes into the snow and earth. The problem arises if you cut two sets of tracks that were not made by bulls. The mistake often made, especially in powder snow, is to guess that a large cow track belongs to a bull.

One quick way to decide is to look at the small track. If it is the track of a small elk, such as a yearling or calf, it is very unlikely that a bull would be traveling with these immature animals. I've been excited many times to cut fresh elk tracks like the above, and I've occasionally made the mistake of letting my enthusiasm get the best of me. The result was always a long, hard hunt that ended when I looked up to find a couple of bald heads staring back at me.

A herd of elk that has been alerted in deep, powdery snow can sometimes be a problem for a hunter. The fine snow falls back into the tracks and it is difficult to decide which tracks belong to a bull. A bull has certain tendencies when he has been alerted with other elk. He will almost always cut out from the rest of the herd at some time and go off on his own. Look for that single track that suddenly leaves the others, and follow it. Usually, it will be a bull.

The hunter who follows a track must move fast at certain times to close the gap, and then slow down to a stalk when he feels the elk might be near. Generally, a bull will look for a ridge to bed down on, and if the track is heading for a nearby ridge, you can move fast in that direction. But when you move to within a couple hundred yards of a potential bedding area, slow way down and begin looking for the elk.

A bull that has seen, heard, or smelled a trailing hunter will break into a trot for about 50 yards and then begin walking again, but much faster this time. If you are following tracks that are just meandering through the forest, but suddenly break into a trot for a short distance, you can bet that the elk somehow detected you. The best thing to do is give up. An elk can cover much more ground at an alerted walk than a hunter will in a day's hunt. And if you kick out a bull, but can't get a shot at it, forget it. That animal will not let you sneak up on him again.

Elk Beds. A hunter who is moving along a ridge will often find fresh elk beds. It is simple to tell which beds were made by bulls upon careful inspection of the beds. After an elk has laid all night in a bed, it stands up and then urinates. A cow will urinate in a splash off the end of her bed, but a bull will urinate in a concentrated stream into his bed.

Fair Weather Hunting. After a heavy snowfall, the weather may clear off. This leaves the snow dry and powdery for days. It is difficult to tell whether an elk track is an hour old or two days old when the snow is fluffy. However, there are a few tricks that can be used to help a hunter judge when the tracks were made. If the snow will not give you any clue about the tracks, follow them until you find some droppings. If the droppings have ice crystals on them, the tracks are old. Also, if the droppings have sunk into the snow due to the radiant energy of the sun warming them up at midday, the tracks are old.

Fair weather also means bitter cold temperatures. The elk must eat much more to generate body heat, and you can expect to find them feeding later into the day and beginning sooner in the afternoon. Also, expect to find the elk bedded down on exposed ridges where they will catch the warming rays of the afternoon sun. Whenever I know that there are elk nearby during cold, sunny days, I always begin glassing those open ridges that catch the sun. You'll find elk more quickly that way than if you neglected the sunlit ridges.

The Migration

The snow in late season eventually builds up until the elk find food scarce. When the snow builds up to about 18 inches, the elk will move down to a lower elevation where the snow is not as deep. This is called the migration. It does not occur like the classic migrations out of Yellowstone National Park where long lines of thousands of elk can be seen in a steady stream snaking down from the high country. Instead, the migration in most elk hunting areas is a slow procession. With each snowfall, the elk move down a little lower and become easier to hunt.

The migration period is the best time to kill a trophy sized bull elk. Even the wiliest of old bulls will be forced to move down from those backcountry thickets that were almost impossible to hunt effectively

A snow depth of 18 inches will force the bulls to move down to a lower elevation where more feed can be found. This is called the migration, but it is a much slower process than the massive migrations in our national parks.

earlier in the season. Also, the elk range in a particular drainage will shrink considerably as deep snow makes the higher, less accessible terrain unsuitable for elk. This favors the hunter, the bull elk seem to know it because they stay as far up in the high country as possible. But now they are susceptible to the efforts of a diligent hunter.

The problem that an elk hunter will encounter when hunting migrating elk is that he can use up his entire hunt tracking cows in the lower elevations and never get up to where the big bulls are living. After the rut, bull elk tend to become solitary animals, or they will travel with other bulls. It is not unusual to find several bulls living together in harmony late in the season.

The first elk to move down when snow begins to build up will be the cows and calves. Spike bulls will also move down with the cows, but the big bulls will linger in the deep snow and move down more grudgingly. As an example, the main elk herd consisting of cows and spikes may have moved down to the 5,000 foot level where the snow is a foot deep, but the trophy sized bulls will stay up at the 6,000 foot elevation where the snow is 18 inches deep.

It is difficuilt for a new elk hunter to move on up the mountain past a profusion of fresh elk sign in the snow, but if a big bull elk is your quarry, you must keep going until you hit the lonely tracks of the mature bulls higher up the mountainside. Every year where I hunt in western Montana, I drive up old logging roads past other hunters who are excitedly examining fresh elk tracks in a foot of snow. I leave them behind to continue in their futile efforts among the cows and calves, and I drive a couple miles higher up the mountain until the four wheel drive jeep can't make it any farther. Then I know that I am in trophy bull elk country.

One nice thing about hunting the migration is that you don't have to keep roaming throughout the country in search of elk. Once you have found an area where the elk are migrating through, you can return to the same area daily and more elk will have moved in overnight. Another benefit when you hunt the same area regularly is that you begin to get a feel for where the elk will pass through and where they will bed down, and you can plan on hunting those areas every morning.

Generally, the best way to hunt migrating bulls in deep snow is to get on a vantage point and glass open sidehills or breaks in the timber. Not only can you glass for elk on a far sidehill, but you can also watch for any new tracks that may have appeared since you last glassed that spot. If no elk are seen in those openings, continue walking until you cut a fresh set of tracks on a ridge and begin following them.

Once again, the one problem area when moving in on a bull elk in deep snow is that the animals always seem to be above you. A bull bedded down on a ridge stands a much better chance of spotting a hunter moving up on him before the hunter sees the elk. This is a lot bigger problem than it seems. The large majority of my unsuccessful encounters with bulls have resulted from this condition, and I now try hard to find another way to approach a bull elk that I suspect is bedded down above me. When I approach a ridge that might have my bull bedded down on it, I leave the tracks a couple hundred yards below the ridge and circle around until I reach the ridgetop. I then slowly hunt down the ridge, and I've shot several bulls in the back of the head from close range while the animals were watching their back trail below.

Special Late Season Hunts On Migration Routes

There are several unique late season elk hunts along major migration routes leading out of Yellowstone National Park. Every winter, beginning in December, thousands of elk stream out of the park because the food supply there is sparse. The elk migrate onto national forest land

***Many mature bulls like this one migrate out of Yellowstone Park and are harvested
by hunters during late season special permit hunts just outside the park.***

and do great damage to private ranch land nearby. As a result, extensive
special late seasons have been created to deal with this problem.

The two most well-known late hunts are the Gardiner and Gallatin
hunts just outside the park boundary in Montana. Each year thousands
of either-sex or antlerless permits are issued for these areas. I have been
in Gardiner when the hunts were going on, and I've been amazed at
the many huge six-point bulls that are harvested in these hunts. Truly,
this is the perfect hunt for the sportsman who is looking for a record
sized bull elk.

The Gardiner hunt offers the most permits because large numbers
of elk migrate past this small town at the park's north entrance. The
area surrounding the park is open or lightly timbered, and migrating
bands of elk can be seen daily moving north out of the park. It is not
difficult to find the elk either. The state of Montana wants those huge
surplus elk herds trimmed and the officer at the local checking station
is always glad to direct elk hunters to areas where elk herds have been
recently spotted.

The Gallatin late season hunt takes place in the Gallatin National Forest west of the town of West Yellowstone on the Park's western boundary. It issues about half the number of permits (usually about 2,000) as the Gardiner hunt. The hunt area is in heavily timbered, steep mountains. The snow is usually deep and this hunt is generally considered more rugged than the Gardiner hunt.

Access in both areas is limited to horseback or walking. However, the state does allow a period at midday when snowmobiles may be used to retrieve downed game.

Success is high, especially in the Gardiner hunt, and most hunters kill an elk. The hunts are broken up into short time periods from two to four days and permitees are issued dates when they can hunt. This eliminates overhunting and congestion and allows a long season, often into February.

Permits for both of these late season hunts must be applied for from the state of Montana when other special permit applications are due in mid-June. It is not difficult to draw a permit due to the large number issued, and any prospective elk hunter who is looking for a unique elk hunt with a good chance for success should consider this hunt.

Another special elk hunt takes place in Wyoming along the southern migration route out of Yellowstone Park, though this hunt begins much earlier—October until mid-November. It is called the Teton elk hunt because much of the hunting is in Teton National Park, along with a corner of the National Elk Refuge.

The Teton elk hunt offers about 450 permits annually to hunters who apply for the unit-79 area. Permit holders are allowed to hunt in other areas of the state before the migration begins. But when the elk begin moving out of the park, permit holders quickly move in for a chance at one of those huge Yellowstone bull elk.

Late Season Safety Concerns

Any sportsman who makes an elk hunt in the western wilderness should be concerned with safety. Every year about a dozen tragedies are reported in the western states, and virtually every death could have been avoided if the hunter had been concerned about his safety and made some provisions for an emergency.

The problems that will be encountered in the backcountry are not the sensational type such as wild animals attacking a hunter, or crazed mountain men descending on camp. Instead, small errors in judgement are what caused critical problems for the unprepared hunter. Small things like a wrong turn hiking back to camp, a twisted ankle five miles from a vehicle, or forgetting matches can quickly grow into desperate situations.

Safety in the mountains can be broken down into two areas—preventive safety and prepared safety. With preventive safety, you do things to keep from putting yourself in danger, and with prepared safety you plan ahead to be ready in case an emergency arises.

If you are serious about staying out of trouble in the mountains, you will carry a compass at all times. Most emergency situations that arise outdoors occur when a hunter gets turned around and is not sure of the direction back to camp or his vehicle. Getting lost is not the killer, but the resulting exposure of an exhausted hunter staying out in the elements overnight is. Hypothermia, the lowering of the body temperature due to exposure, is the number one killer of lost hunters.

You may never have to use a compass, but if you should ever need one, a compass can save your life as sure as a rescue team. And you don't have to acquire the compass knowledge of an expert. If you are going into an area where no easy landmarks are apparent, take a compass reading before you leave the road. Then if you get turned around, you will know for sure which compass reading will take you back to the road. It's as simple as that, yet lives are lost every year because a compass was not used at the beginning of the day.

Fear is the next subject of preventive safety. Most lost hunters are dressed well enough to stay alive through a night of below freezing temperatures in the mountains, and in the morning they can usually figure out how to get back to camp. But only if they can maintain a safe body temperature. A hunter who realizes that he is lost will feel the urge to panic over his unknown position, and that is the beginning of the end for him. He will expend all of his stored energy which would have kept his body temperature up during the night, and he will perspire profusely until his clothing is drenched in sweat. The result is a man huddled under a tree slowly freezing to death in his own sweat.

Fear and panic for the lost hunter are natural reactions, but a man can condition himself to act rationally when he gets turned around in the mountains. The best way to fight fear and panic is to think about what you would do if you were lost *before* that situation arises. This is a good subject to talk about around the campfire. It's almost like a conditioned response. When you get lost, your mind will turn back to the sober thinking that you did on the matter, and you will have a sensible plan to get back safe before fear and panic get the chance to cloud your thinking.

If you should get lost, you have lost only half the battle, because if you have prepared for such an occasion, you will live to hunt another day. Every year hundreds of hunters fail to find their way back home at the end of the day, but they spend a moderately comfortable night in the mountains because they prepared for exactly that type of emergency.

The lost hunter will need two things—food and shelter. With these in his possession, any man can spend a night in the forest and come out the next day in good condition. And with innovations in lightweight emergency foods and space blankets, an excellent emergency pack does not have to weigh more than a few pounds.

I carry at all times an assortment of tasty dried foods and juice, waterproof matches for a fire, and a space blanket to huddle under just in case I get turned around at the end of the day or break a leg and can't make it out of the forest that night. This stuff can simply be packed in with the other utensils that you carry for field dressing an elk. It doesn't matter how you put your emergency pack together or where you carry it, just make sure you don't start any day elk hunting without one.

One more safety concern is snowblindness, or sunglare. During those bright sunny days when the snow glistens, a hunter may begin to feel sick to his stomach in the afternoon and develop a severe headache. His eyes will feel dry and tender. These are the symptoms of sunglare. A pair of sunglasses will solve this problem. I wear photogray prescription lenses that darken when the sun is bright, and lighten in the shadows.

Archery Hunting The Late Season

A unique and very enjoyable way to hunt elk with bow and arrow is in the late season when cold weather and deep snow grip the mountains. A few western states offer late season archery hunts, and while the archery success rate is not high, there is a great deal of pleasure to be had. Even the trophy standards of an archer change under the hardships of bowhunting in winter. A cow or spike bull that might have been passed up in the early archery season are now pursued with fervor and claimed as trophies.

The late season archer must adapt his hunting style to follow that of the late season rifle hunter. He must look for migrating elk herds and glass open feeding areas for elk. However, the archer who will go after cows and spike bulls will find those animals at lower elevations and sometimes even within sight of driveable roads. The first late season elk that I killed was a cow elk that died within 300 yards of the freeway in northern Idaho.

An archer still must make a careful stalk to get within bow range of an elk, but the animals at this time of year are not overly cautious, and a successful stalk even through sparse cover is possible. White camouflage will spell the difference between success and failure during a stalk on elk through the snow. I use a pair of white painter's coveralls, a white stocking cap with facemask, and gray ski gloves. The elk look

Dressed in white camouflage, Mike Lapinski stands an excellent chance of making a successful stalk on an elk in the snow during a late season archery hunt.

right through you when you use white camo, and you can even stalk across open areas directly in an elk's line of vision if you move very slowly.

The one item that changes noticeably for an archer from early season to late season is his bow's performance. A bow will act sluggish when the temperature is zero. At 10 yards, you may not notice the difference, but at 30 yards, your arrows will consistently hit almost a foot below the target. Remember to place your sight pin a little high on an elk to compensate for this drop.

6

The Elk
Hunting Rifle

There have been a million words written in search of the perfect caliber for hunting elk. Everything from the 6mm up to the .460 Weatherby Magnum has entered the discussion. But alas, there is no *perfect* caliber. Many will do the job of killing an elk depending on range, shot placement, etc., but a few within a certain range will do the job most dependably.

Bullet speed alone does not kill an elk; neither does bullet weight. The .22-.250 screams along at almost 4,000 fps (feet per second), and the .35 Remington lobs a heafty 200-grain bullet, but neither is a good elk gun. The .22-.250 doesn't have enough bullet weight when it gets to an elk, and the .35 is going too slow if it ever gets there!

Instead, it is the combination of bullet speed and weight that causes the damage that kills the elk. When you combine both forces, you end up with energy measured in footpounds. It's what we hunters commonly call "knock down power."

That's what the serious elk hunter should be looking for in a rifle caliber—the combination of bullet speed and weight that hits an elk with such a thunderous wallop that the huge brute goes down and stays down.

The most popular calibers that have proven adequate for elk hunting are the .270 Winchester, 7mm Remington Magnum, .308 Winchester, .30-06 Springfield, .300 Winchester Magnum and .338 Winchester Magnum. There are a host of other calibers squeezed in between these, including such favorites as the .280 Remington and the Weatherby

Magnums, but since the six calibers listed are the most popular, we'll limit our primary discussion to them.

The .270 Winchester

Many hunters and guides consider the .270 too light for elk. They may have a point, but the credentials of the .270 in certain situations cannot be denied.

The .270 is an adequate elk caliber because its oversize case contains enough powder to push a 150-grain bullet into the 3,000 fps range. The retained energy at 400 yards is nearly 1,200 ft/lbs, which is plenty to ruin any bull elk's day with a well placed shot. The .270 was the famous Jack O'Connor's favorite elk rifle, and for the skilled hunter it still has its place today. But because the heaviest bullet available is the 150-grain, hunters looking for a specialized elk rifle will probably pass on the .270 and opt for a caliber that offers a heavier bullet and more retained energy.

Reported Ballistics For Factory-loaded .270 Winchester
(150-grain bullet fired from a 24-inch test barrel)

Range (yds)	Velocity (fps)	Energy (ft/lbs)
muzzle	2,850	2,705
100	2,500	2,085
200	2,180	1,585
300	1,890	1,185
400	1,620	870
500	1,390	640

Trajectory
(for a rifle zeroed at 200 yards)

Range (yds)	Bullet location from line of sight (ins)
muzzle	− 1.5
50	+ 0.9
100	+ 2.0
150	+ 1.8
200	0.0
300	− 9.4
400	− 28.6
500	− 61.3

The 7mm Remington Magnum

Someone in a musty old gunshop must have heard the gripe about the .270, because the 7mm Magnum came along with a slightly larger case that could hold enough powder to push a 175-grain slug faster than the .270 could move its lighter bullet.

That means the 175-grain bullet from the 7mm Magnum retains nearly 2,000 ft/lbs at 400 yards. Bullet drop is about 42 inches. Better than the .270 without a lot more recoil.

Minimal bullet drop and adequate knock down power at the extreme range are its credentials. The 7mm Remington Magnum is an elk gun—a very good elk gun.

Reported Ballistics For Factory-loaded 7mm Remington Magnum
(175-grain bullet fired from a 24-inch test barrel)

Range (yds)	Velocity (fps)	Energy (ft/lbs)
muzzle	2,860	3,220
100	2,650	2,720
200	2,440	2,310
300	2,240	1,960
400	2,060	1,640
500	1,880	1,370

Trajectory
(for a rifle zeroed at 200 yards)

Range (yds)	Bullet location from line of sight (ins)
muzzle	− 1.5
50	+ 0.7
100	+ 1.7
150	+ 1.5
200	0.0
300	− 7.6
400	−22.1
500	−44.9

The .308 Winchester

The .308 has the bullet speed and weight to closely match the legendary .30-06 at shorter ranges. Many hunters like the .308 in areas where shots at elk will usually be at 200 yards or less, but beyond that range bullet drop will begin to present problems.

In the .308 loading, a 180-grain bullet will retain over 1200 ft/lbs at 400 yards, but the bullet will have dropped some 52 inches. That's a big amount to deal with, especially if the target is moving.

One advantage of the .308 is that it can be chambered in a short action turnbolt rifle. This makes it a popular caliber in the synthetic-stocked, lightweight "mountain rifles" which are all the rage. For the hunter who'll carry his rifle from sunrise to sunset to find trophy class bulls in rugged terrain, that's a real plus.

Reported Ballistics For Factory-loaded .308 Winchester
(180-grain bullet fired from a 24-inch test barrel)

Range (yds)	Velocity (fps)	Energy (ft/lbs)
muzzle	2,620	2,745
100	2,390	2,290
200	2,180	1,895
300	1,970	1,555
400	1,780	1,270
500	1,600	1,030

Trajectory
(for a rifle zeroed at 200 yards)

Range (yds)	Bullet location from line of sight (ins)
muzzle	− 1.5
50	+ 1.1
100	+ 2.3
150	+ 2.0
200	0.0
300	− 9.7
400	−28.3
500	−57.9

The .30-06 Springfield

The .30-06 has had a long and auspicious history that we don't need to go into here. Suffice it to say that is far and away the most popular "all-around" big game rifle caliber. Year after year the .30-06 shows up near the top of the charts for reloading die sales.

For the hunter who will use the same rifle to hunt everything from moose on down to the occasional prairie dog, the .30-06 is probably the best choice. The choice of bullet weights ranges from 110 grains up to 220 grains.

Loaded with its most popular bullet for elk hunting, the 180-grain, the .30-06 will retain 1,300+ ft/lbs at 400 yards. That's plenty to knock a bull off his feet! However, bullet drop remains nearly 50 inches. Bullet drop is a problem that plagues most of the .30 caliber cartridges.

Because of its great popularity, the .30-06 offers another advantage. It is available in almost every action and in virtually every brand of firearm. You'll have no problem in finding a rifle action, model and style to suit you. And if you head into the boondocks, but leave the ammunition on the kitchen table, you'll have no problem buying or borrowing for the .30-06.

Reported Ballistics For Factory-loaded .30-06 Springfield
(180-grain bullet fired from a 24-inch test barrel)

Range (yds)	Velocity (fps)	Energy (ft/lbs)
muzzle	2,700	2,915
100	2,470	2,435
200	2,250	2,025
300	2,040	1,665
400	1,850	1,360
500	1,660	1,105

Trajectory
(for a rifle zeroed at 200 yards)

Range (yds)	Bullet location from line of sight (ins)
muzzle	− 1.5
50	+ 0.9
100	+ 2.1
150	+ 1.8
200	0.0
300	− 8.9
400	− 26.2
500	− 54.0

The .300 Winchester Magnum

Serious sportsmen who do a lot of elk hunting often choose the .300 Magnum. This mighty caliber pushes a 200-grain bullet to 400 yards and still retains 2200+ fps velocity and 2200+ ft/lbs of energy! Muzzle velocity is greater with a 220-grain bullet than many other "elk" calibers that are restricted to lighter bullets! With the .300 Winchester

Magnum in hand, a hunter need never wonder if his bullet will have enough authority even if he must reach 450 yards across a canyon with it.

A hunter in the market for a "strictly elk" rifle couldn't do much better than the .300 Magnum. That is, if he isn't bothered by recoil. The .300 lives up to its designation as a "magnum" at both ends of the rifle. Because of the kick, the .300 Magnum is often chambered in heavy, long-barreled rifles that can be a bother to carry all day.

Reported Ballistics For Factory-loaded .300 Winchester Magnum
(180-grain bullet fired from a 24-inch test barrel)

Range (yds)	Velocity (fps)	Energy (ft/lbs)
muzzle	2,960	3,500
100	2,750	3,010
200	2,540	2,580
300	2,340	2,195
400	2,160	1,860
500	1,980	1,565

Trajectory
(for a rifle zeroed at 200 yards)

Range (yds)	Bullet location from line of sight (ins)
muzzle	− 1.5
50	+ 0.6
100	+ 1.5
150	+ 1.4
200	0.0
300	− 7.0
400	− 20.3
500	− 41.0

The .338 Winchester Magnum

The .338 Magnum is an elk gun. Besides the occasional moose, it isn't good for much of the other game that lives in the lower 48 states. Bullet weights begin at 200 grains and end at 300 grains. In fact, ballistics tables show the .338 Magnum has *more* power than needed to kill an elk.

Even so, the .338 Magnum has become a popular caliber among serious elk hunters, especially those who make an occasional hunting trip for game animals like bear that hunt back.

There are some good reasons for choosing the .338 as an elk caliber.

First, knock down power even at extreme ranges cannot be denied. Enthusiasts note that a less-than-perfect shot on a bull elk at 400 yards with a .338 will still drop it fast! Secondly, bullet stability is very good. The velocity of the heavy 250 grain bullet will not drop off as quickly as that of lighter bullets traveling the same speed. And the heavy bullet isn't as susceptible to wind drift.

The numbers *are* awesome. At 400 yards that big bullet is still traveling at something around 2000 fps! Energy is still more than 2000 ft/lbs.

The recoil is *awesome* too! Some hunters say as much as three times the .270 which was on the bottom end of our scale! For comfort and accuracy, rifles chambered for .338 Magnum usually weigh in the 8 to 10 pound range. That's a lot more than I want to carry in the mountains unless I'm hunting from horseback.

Reported Ballistics For Factory-loaded .338 Winchester Magnum
(210-grain bullet fired from a 24-inch test barrel)

Range (yds)	Velocity (fps)	Energy (ft/lbs)
muzzle	2,830	3,735
100	2,590	3,130
200	2,370	2,610
300	2,150	2,155
400	1,940	1,760
500	1,750	1,435

Trajectory
(for a rifle zeroed at 200 yards)

Range (yds)	Bullet location from line of sight (ins)
muzzle	− 1.5
50	+ 0.8
100	+ 1.8
150	+ 1.6
200	0.0
300	− 8.0
400	− 23.7
500	− 48.6

Which Firearm Is For You?

Selection of an elk hunting gun, including the caliber, depends on how serious you are about elk hunting. If a man from upstate New York

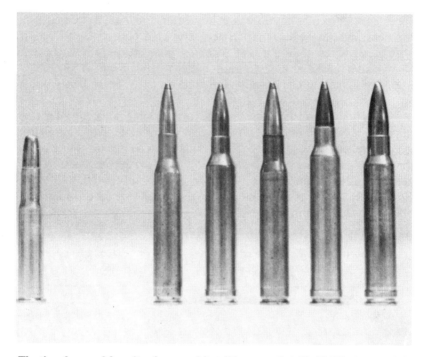

The time-honored favorite of many whitetail hunters, the .30-.30 Winchester, (left) is dwarfed by the five most popular elk hunting calibers on the right. They are: (from left) .270 Winchester, 7mm Remington Magnum, .30-06 Springfield, .300 Winchester Magnum and .338 Winchester Magnum. These calibers, for the most part, have the powder capacity and the right bullet weights to give real knock down power for long range elk shooting.

is planning a once-in-a-lifetime elk hunt and he already has a .30-06 pump or auto in his gun cabinet, he probably need not look any further for the right gun for his elk hunting trip. That same gun he has used with 150-grain bullets to hunt whitetails will be adequate for elk with 180-grain bullets.

For the hunter whose passion is elk, a more specialized rifle is in order. The dedicated elk hunter can't go wrong with the .300 Winchester Magnum in a top quality turnbolt, maybe even a custom rig. As discussed, recoil is there, but not excessive and the tremendous velocities of the .300 Magnum's heavy bullets make it an elk-dropper at ranges even beyond 400 yards if necessary.

Rifle Design

If you are planning to purchase a new rifle for your elk hunting trip, choose a bolt action. Rigidity of the action, simplicity and speed of firing pin fall, and precise breeching which supports the entire cartridge make the bolt action the most accurate and reliable.

Brand and model of the chosen rifle are not nearly as important as being comfortable with the gun and having confidence in it. That only comes with practice and proper sighting in.

In selecting an elk rifle, consider synthetic-stocked models. In most cases this is a feature that must be added after a rifle is purchased, but riflemakers including Remington, Winchester, Sako and Weatherby are offering this option on new guns.

Synthetic stocks, usually of some type of Fiberglas construction, offer the elk hunter a good number of advantages. First, they are tough. They'll take a beating and show nary a sign of having been out of the scabbard. Second, they are light; a real advantage when you're hunting on foot in rugged terrain. Third, they are impervious to weather. Temperature and humidity play havoc with wooden stocks, opening and closing the pores in the wood and affecting the accuracy of the gun. You can soak a synthetic stock in a creek overnight, and it won't change a thing.

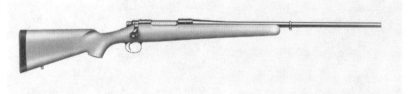

If you're buying a rifle specifically for elk hunting, one like this may get the nod. It's a bolt action, is available in a number of popular elk calibers, and sports a synthetic stock. This particular gun is a Remington 700 Custom KS Mountain rifle.

If your new rifle didn't come with swivels and a sling, see that it gets them. Don't skimp on the sling. Be sure you get one that's comfortable. If you don't on your first trip, you will on your second.

Top the rifle with a *quality* scope! While some hunters still prefer the simplicity of a fixed 4-power, today's variables in the 2-7 or 3-9 ranges are hard to beat. Whatever your selection, buy the best scope you can afford! Good lenses and good coatings can give you 10 or 15 minutes of extra shooting light on either end of the day. You will quickly find out how important that can be when a trophy bull is bugling just inside the edge of the timber at dusk and you can't find him in your scope!

Sighting In Your Rifle

Any hunter planning an elk hunt should have his rifle sighted-in for

In elk country, long range shots and poor light conditions are the norm. A power-ful, flat-shooting rifle equipped with a quality scope is the proper tool. Be sure that you practice enough to be really confident in your rig.

long range shooting. Not only that, he should also do some long range shooting practice. In addition, he should begin estimating long range distances so that he will be better able to figure out how far away a bull is on a distant sidehill.

I grew up in the oak forests of Pennsylvania. Shots at deer averaged 50 yards. A 100-yard shot was unusual, and usually missed. The standard sighting-in method was to put a 12-inch pie plate out at 50 yards. If I hit it, my rifle was sighted in. For western elk hunting, that's not good enough. Any shooter can sight in his rifle well enough to kill an elk at 400 yards if he follows the proper sighting-in method.

Bore-sight your rifle first. Set up a solid bench rest 25 yards from the target and pull the bolt from your rifle. Look through the bore and center it on the bullseye. Then look through the scope and move the crosshairs until they rest on the bullseye also. A special bore-sighting device is especially convenient and allows you to accomplish this task at home without wasting your time at the range. This will save many wasted shots when sighting-in a new rifle or scope.

Your first shot should be from 25 yards, and you want the bullet to hit a half inch below dead center. The bullet must rise about 1.5 inches from bore to scope level to hit the target at 25 yards, and it will continue to rise to about three inches high at 100 yards in the caliber range we're talking about.

Now for the fine tuning. Set your solid bench rest at 100 yards and see where your group is. You will have to do some fine adjusting to get a perfect group, but once your rifle is consistently putting holes three inches above the bullseye at 100 yards, you can be sure that it will hit an elk at 400 yards.

The bullet drop at long range varies slightly with each caliber. Check the ballistics for your rifle and know how much drop it has at 400 yards. The nice thing about sighting-in three inches high is that your bullet will not have dropped enough up to 300 yards to have to worry about it.

One word of caution. Many new elk hunters miss the long range shot because they hold *too high* over the back of an elk. For instance, a hunter who shoots a .30-06 decides that at 400 yards he should hold a foot above an elk's back. It is nearly impossible to judge when the crosshairs are 12 inches above the elk's back at that distance. The result is that a hunter often holds five feet high and overshoots the elk—even at 400 yards!

Experienced elk hunters sight in their rifles to have no more than 30 inches drop at 400 yards. That way, they need only place the crosshairs on the top of the back to make a deadly chest shot.

Windage consideration is vital when shooting at long range. A bullet that reaches across a 400 yard span will be blown off course to some degree, depending on the weight of the bullet and wind speed. This was never more apparent than when a client of mine took a long shot at a huge bull elk.

This man had supreme confidence in his .30-06 and informed me that he could kill any elk at 400 yards. After several tough hunts, we finally found a bull feeding with several cows across a drainage. From prior hunts, I knew the distance to be about 385 yards. My client took two shots at the bull and missed both times.

To properly sight your rifle, you must shoot from a solid, well-padded rest.

We checked where the bull was standing and found where both of his bullets had plowed into the earth at the correct elevation, but were about two feet to the right—just enough to miss the elk. That got me looking into wind drift. I was amazed at my findings. A 180-grain bullet from a .30-06 will have a wind drift of 45 inches at 400 yards in a 20 mph cross wind!

It's tricky making a windage allowance. However, shooting at long range often does not spook an elk, and you may have several shots at the animal. If you have a good hold, but continue to miss, take note of the wind and compensate slightly for it.

Bullet Weight And Composition

Occasionally, a hunter will make a perfect shot on an elk, but the animal will go a long way before dying. I once had a hunter recount an experience during which he shot a bull elk with a .300 Magnum at 80 yards. The bullet hit a rib and penetrated only far enough to destroy

As these Hornady posters exhibit, there are many bullet types available from a single manufacturer. Consider carefully the weight and construction of the bullet you choose for elk loads.

one lung. Luckily, the guy was able to track the bull down in fresh snow. This hunter was adamant that the .300 Magnum was not a good elk rifle.

The .300 Magnum *is* an excellent elk gun. The problem was the hunter's bullet selection. He was using a 150-grain bullet with a thin jacket. At 80 yards the bullet was screaming along at 3100 fps. When it hit a rib, the thin copper jacket could not hold the lead core together, and the bullet disintegrated into tiny fragments.

Bullet weight and composition are critical ingredients in the overall performance of your hunting rifle. The elk hunting gun will have high velocity performance, and this tends to make a bullet fragment unless its composition allows a controlled expansion. It doesn't make sense to take a gun such as the .300 Magnum and shoot a lighter bullet at supersonic speed. A heavier bullet will deliver just as much, probably more knock down power, and the bullet's weight will make it more stable.

Bullet composition is critical for controlled expansion. The perfect bullet peels back into a mushroom-like blob, thereby creating more damage as the bullet moves through the elk. In the past, not enough attention was given to controlled expansion. Bullets on the market today, however, provide excellent expansion in both handloads and factory loads.

Two bullets to keep in mind are the Nosler Partition and the Speer Grand Slam. The Partition bullet has a solid copper partition in the middle. The front half of the bullet expands until it reaches the copper partition. The rear half of the bullet still has enough mass to keep the mushroomed half moving forward instead of fragmenting. The Partition bullet is available in factory manufactured loads.

The handloader should consider the Grand Slam. This bullet has a copper jacket whose thickness varies from thin at the tip of the bullet to heavy towards the base. The result is a thin jacket at the tip which quickly peels back upon impact, allowing proper mushroom expansion. The heavy jacket at the base of the bullet keeps the expansion under control and maintains weight at the base to keep the bullet plowing forward.

7

Bowhunting Gear
For The Elk Hunter

Although there are just as many, possibly more, brands and models of equipment for the bowhunter to choose from, his decisions aren't nearly as complicated as those of the rifle hunter. That simplicity of gear and sport is one of the reasons so many NAHC members and other hunters are turning to the bow and arrow.

This isn't to say that the elk hunter who chooses archery doesn't have any decisions to make! Not by a long shot. Though he doesn't have to worry about caliber, action, scope power and the like, he needs to find a bow that fits him, the arrows to match it, broadheads in which he has confidence and any other paraphernalia that will make it easier to hit and kill an elk.

Bows

Elk are huge animals and a bowhunter must use a bow with a heavy draw weight to insure deep penetration. The best blood trails are usually from an animal through which a broadhead-tipped arrow has passed completely. It takes some power to do that on a big bull with a less than perfect shot.

The ideal peak draw weight for an elk hunting bow is around 65 pounds, with a 60-pound pull about minimum. Sure, there have been elk killed with bows drawing at lower weights when perfect shots were made, but the heavier bows will have the power to punch an arrow through the shoulder blade if your shot is slightly off.

To be successful, the bowhunter must have thorough knowledge of his equipment.
He is working under a set of self-imposed limitations which require confidence
in one's equipment and oneself.

Heavier draw weight bows into the 70-, 80-, and 90-pound range are fine, *if you can handle them*. It is far more important that you be able to shoot your bow accurately than get some kind of ego trip for having the highest draw weight in camp. With practice, virtually every adult hunter can draw a 60- or 65-pound compound or cam and hold it steady.

The type of bow is not vital so long as it meets the legal requirements of the state in which you are hunting. It can be a long bow, recurve, compound or cam bow so long as it has the draw weight to handle the job of penetrating a tough old bull.

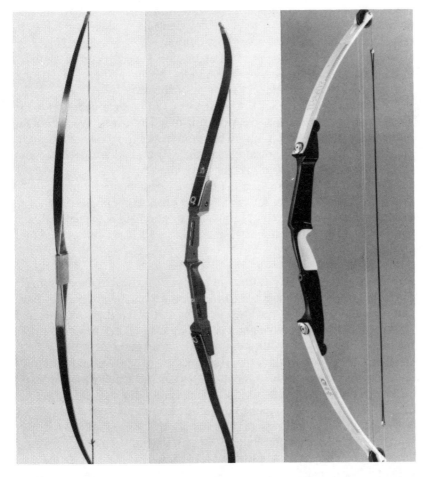

From left to right, these photos represent the progression from long bow to recurve bow to compound bow. All can be, and still are, used to take elk.

Far and away, the most popular hunting bows today are the compound and cam models from a long list of quality manufacturers. As the general popularity of bowhunting continues to increase, so will the popularity of these bows. They have the greatest arrow speeds which means flatter trajectory to longer ranges. That take some of the guess work out of range estimation which many hunters find so difficult. Compound and cam bows also offer draw weight reduction which makes it possible for hunters of smaller stature to shoot the heavier draw weights. That feature is infinitely useful when a bull decides to take his sweet time coming out from behind a cow that's blocking your line of fire!

Recurve bows have seen a resurgence in popularity because many hunters get into archery for the simplicity of it. Recurves are mechanically very simple and very lightweight. They don't have wheels or cables to tangle in tree limbs, and about the only maintenance required is a new string now and then. For the hunter on horseback, recurves come in a number of takedown versions for easier carrying and packing. That's a real bonus when hunting in timber and brush.

What the muzzleloader is to the modern rifle, the longbow is to the compound bow. It takes a great deal of practice just to learn to draw, aim and shoot one. The hunter who chooses the longbow for his archery hunting does so for nostalgia and the added challenge, not because it is the most efficient tool available to him.

More so than for the rifle hunter, the bowhunter is quite likely to find the same bow he uses for whitetails or other medium-sized big game will work very well for elk. Not having to purchase a specialized bow is one way in which an archery hunt can be a savings over a rifle hunt!

Arrows

Arrow size and composition are not overly critical to the elk hunter. For size, go with the recommendations of the manufacturers. They have complete listings of what arrows work best at given draw weights and lengths. Fiberglas, graphite and cedar shafts are all available, but most hunting today is done with aluminum shaft arrows.

You can use top-of-the-line arrows or less expensive shafts and kill elk with either. However, if you're doing as much practicing as you should be for your elk hunt, harder anodized aluminum shafts will last longer. They'll also be on the expensive end of the scale.

Coloration of the arrow shaft is important. They should blend well with the forest background, but not so well that you can't find one after you shoot it! Two-tone camouflaged arrows are fine, as long as the fletches and nocks are a fluorescent color which can be easily spotted against grass or leaves. It is also helpful to use glow-in-the-dark nocks on these

Mike Lapinski prefers Autumn XX75 shafts with brightly colored fletches and nocks. They are easy to find after a shot and show blood sign better than dark colored shafts.

arrows which make them easier to find with a flashlight after dark. *Finding your arrow is crucial to your ability to judge the placement of your hit, or determine if you hit the elk at all!*

I like Easton's XX75 shaft in autumn orange. This color seems to blend in well with the surroundings, but it is easy to spot after a shot. Blood sign is also easier to read on these lighter colored shafts.

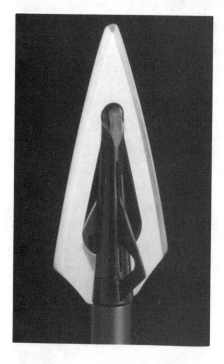

Because elk are heavy-hided and heavy-boned animals, many hunters prefer broadheads that have a cutting, leading edge. One such head is the Bear Super Razorhead.

Broadheads

No matter what type, brand or model broadhead the elk hunter selects, it must be razor sharp! Unlike the rifle hunter whose projectile kills primarily by shock, secondarily by tissue damage, the bowhunter's kill is caused by hemorrhaging, which is the result of tissue damage caused by the cutting edges of a sharp broadhead. The sharper the edge, the more damage, the greater the hemorrhaging, the faster the kill.

Strength of construction and materials is vitally important to a good broadhead. Size is secondary.

Broadheads that are used to kill deer can be used to kill an elk. However, the heavy hide and larger bones of an elk will sometimes cause the thin blades of some presharpened broadheads to snap off. Solid blades are usually stronger, but some hunters find them more prone to wind

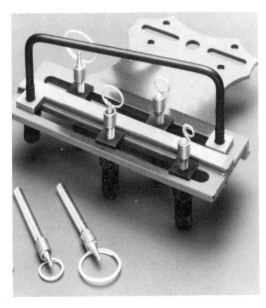

Serious bowhunters will want to consider sights and a whole bunch of other gear. All will be covered in a future book from the NAHC Hunter's Information Series.

planing than heads with vented blades. It comes down to a matter of personal choice and which type you feel most confident with.

Choose a broadhead that has a foolproof locking system for its insertable blades. Make sure the blades are heavy, thick steel, and razor sharp. Then rest assured that this head will be able to do its deadly work when the time comes.

One-piece broadheads are also fine for elk hunting. In the past, this type of broadhead had to be hand sharpened, and most bowhunters had difficulty putting a razor sharp edge on the blades. It is a skill which takes practice to master. However, recently some one-piece broadhead makers have begun offering their one-piece heads with pre-sharpened blades.

Whichever broadhead you choose, it is important that you practice shooting with the head. Serious hunters will shoot nothing but broadheads for several weeks before the season to get the feel of how they fly compared to target or field points. Special targets and practice broadheads are available to make this kind of practice safe and economical.

Other Bowhunting Gear

The bowhunter's basics are bow, arrows and broadheads. They are what he must have to take an elk. However, there are many other pieces of equipment that will make it a more enjoyable experience and turn the odds in the hunter's favor. These include a quiver, sights, a rangefinder, a release, string silencers, arrow rests and a whole list of other gadgets which will be covered in depth by author Glenn Helgeland in another volume of the NAHC Hunter's Information Series.

8

Clothing & Other Gear

The Early Bow Season (September)

September in the West is usually balmy, with temperatures at mid-day in the 80s and cool mornings. However, a storm front can rapidly move in and bring with it rain or snow. The hunter should prepare to wear mostly warm weather clothes, but he should also bring along enough of the proper clothing for rain or snow conditions.

Most hunting done for elk in September is with the bow, and archers usually wear a long sleeve shirt, with their camo clothing worn over that during fair weather. This is enough to keep a hunter warm during the brisk early morning hours, but not too much to overheat him in the afternoon.

A weather front that brings rain in September will also bring cooler temperatures. A good set of rain pants and jacket are a necessity for any hunter planning an elk hunt because a storm system may move in and it could rain every day for a week. In fact, it is vital that a bowhunter is out there hunting in his rain gear in wet weather. I've killed five of my 10 bowkilled elk when it was raining.

An early season snow storm in September is a common occurrence in the West. The snow usually melts within a few days, and the weather returns to normal. A hunter should bring a set of wool clothes so that he can take advantage of the good hunting following a snow storm. A light wool shirt and wool pants will allow a hunter to move in comfort in the snow.

Footwear should include a pair of light leather boots for fair weather, uninsulated rubber boots for wet weather, and insulated rubber boots for snow. Many archers use tennis shoes for silent movement through the forest when the weather is warm and dry.

The Early Rifle Season (October)

Expect cold weather in October. Snow usually does not cover the ground at the beginning of October, but by the end of the month, snow is common. The early October hunter should bring a set of wool clothes, including wool shirt, pants, and long johns, along with a wool jacket. But he should also bring a set of light cotton hunting clothes. That way he can interchange his hunting outfit depending on the weather. If the temperature is 20 degrees but clear, he can skip the heavy wool pants and wear long johns and cotton pants.

Later in the month when snow is on the ground, wear wool. Those heavy wool pants will keep you warm, and they will shed the snow without absorbing moisture. A goose down vest is acceptable during cold weather, but avoid other goose down garments when snow hunting because down loses its insulating quality when it gets wet.

A bowhunter in October has a problem. Temperatures below freezing are common, and an archer must wear enough clothes to keep warm, while still keeping himself camouflaged. A bowhunter can dress adequately by wearing camouflage that is a size larger than normal. That way, he can wear long johns and an extra wool shirt underneath his camo clothes without restricting movement or circulation.

Footgear should include insulated leather boots for cold or dry hunting conditions, and insulated rubber boots for hunting in the snow.

The Late Season (November)

Expect deep snow and cold temperatures in November. Wool clothes should be worn, and that includes long johns, socks, pants, shirt and coat. A hunter can spend all day moving through snow covered brush and tree limbs, but still stay warm and dry with wool.

The late season hunter often is in a quandary to wear the proper clothes during a day's hunt. Bitter cold, below zero temperatures are not uncommon in the mountains, and the cold quickly seeps through a hunter who is wearing a wool jacket if he is standing still for hours watching an open area. But if he wears extra clothing, he will perspire too much when he begins to struggle through the snow. That's where a goosedown vest is valuable. A hunter can wear the vest while he is on stand, and then put it in his pack when he begins moving.

Footgear should include a good pair of insulated rubber boots for

Early season bowhunting calls for clothes that can adapt for early morning chill and mid-day heat. A couple long sleeve shirts and a camo sweater are about right.

The Air-Bob sole is great for gripping frozen snow on steep terrain.

hunting. Bring along a pair of leather insulated boots for wearing around camp.

Boots for Snow Hunting

Steep, mountainous terrain is difficult to walk on when there is snow on the ground. Nonresident elk hunters who are accustomed to wearing insulated rubber boots back home where the ground is flat, discover that the light ripple grip of their boots will not hold on the steep slopes.

A new grip has been offered in recent years that works well on frozen, snow covered ground that is steep. It is called the Air-Bob sole. Tiny, bullet-like projections stick out from the sole and heel of the boot to individually grip the ground. This is an invention directed towards the western sportsman, and the Air-Bob sole is found mostly in western sporting goods stores. However, a nonresident can purchase a pair of boots with Air-Bob soles in any western city where sporting goods are sold.

Backpacks

Each hunter on a self-guided elk hunting trip will need two packs. One to carry his field gear, and one to carry elk quarters. It is not ad-

Fanny packs are small and quiet, yet accommodate everything the elk hunter needs to include in his day pack.

visable to try to accomplish both with one pack. A hunter will break his back trying to pack an elk quarter with a soft backpack, and a backpack with frame is too bulky and noisy for carrying while hunting.

A backpack of sturdy waterproof material with padded shoulder straps is best when hunting. This pack will hold all the field dressing knives, saws, hatchets and game bags, plus food and a survival kit. Consequently, it should fit well because the hunter will have it on his back every minute he is hunting.

Some sportsmen have a problem with backpacks. After a few hours, the steady pull of the straps on their shoulders becomes painful. An alternative to a shoulder pack is a fanny pack. Fanny packs are now made large enough to hold everything that a hunter will need in the field.

Most hunters who make self-guided hunts do not have the luxury of horses to pack out game. They must pack out the animal on their backs, and a good pack frame is vital for this exhausting chore. It's tough enough packing out elk quarters with a good pack frame, but it's murder if you use a cheap one.

A good pack frame is expensive, but it will pay for itself with one pack. A good frame should be constructed with welded aluminum tubing. Wide, well-padded shoulder straps are important, along with a pad-

The self-guided backpack hunt calls for a special individual, and special equipment to match.

ded waist strap which takes much of the load off the shoulders.

Special Gear For Self-Guided Hunts

The hunter who makes a self-guided elk hunt must be sure that his equipment is adequate. Time spent correcting inadequacies in equipment choice and quality will mean less hunting time. Basically, a hunter should bring enough equipment to provide food, warmth, and shelter.

Shelter is important. If you can't keep out the elements, your dream trip will be a miserable experience. A camper trailer or motor home is fine if you have one. Otherwise, a tent must be used. And not just one tent, but two.

Hunters make the mistake of bringing one tent out West to live in for two weeks under a variety of weather conditions. Rain and snow make clothes wet, and with one tent there is nowhere to dry them. And the cooking chore that was planned for outside is a real ordeal if the weather turns nasty. Smart hunters bring along two sturdy tents. One tent is used for sleeping. The other tent is used for cooking and hanging out wet clothes to dry.

A source of heat will be needed for the cook tent. A small sheet metal wood stove is one option, but finding dry wood is often a problem. A kerosene heater is a good alternative. It will put out plenty of heat to keep the tent warm and clothes dry, and you can keep it burning during the day while you are hunting. Don't expect to heat your cook tent with the cook stove. It does not put out enough heat to keep the tent warm, and it will be impossible to dry out damp clothing.

Bathing Facilities

It doesn't matter whether you hunt in the heat of September or the bitter cold of November, you will perspire profusely during the hunt. A daily bath is necessary, and it is surprisingly easy to refresh yourself with a bath or shower even in frigid weather.

The early season hunter does not have too much problem bathing. He can purchase a commercial shower bag that is filled with water and then heated by the sun, or he can simply rig up a primitive shower using a pail hung from a tree with some holes poked into its bottom. Simply heat some water, pour it into the shower pail, and quickly scrub up.

A shower is impossible in November when deep snow and cold are waiting outside the tent. A hunter will have to take a sponge bath. Water is heated and poured into a low, wide tub, and the person crouches down in it and washes himself with a sponge. This can be done in a corner of the warm cook tent without much discomfort to the bather.

Sleeping Bags

A good sleeping bag is essential. It will not only provide warmth, but it will also provide comfortable sleep at night. A bag with a minimum five pounds of fill (about -10 degree rating) will be needed even in the early season. It may get up to 80 degrees at mid-day in September, but fall nights in the mountains are brisk. Bring a thick sponge pad to place under the sleeping bag to make your bed softer, and place a plastic ground cloth under it to keep moisture from seeping up from the earth.

What To Take

Below is a general list of camping equipment needed for a party of three hunters:

☐ 2-tents (10x10)
☐ 1-Coleman cook stove
☐ 3-sets of eating utensils
☐ 1-portable table & chairs
☐ 2-gas lanterns
☐ 1-heating stove
☐ 1-large basin for sponge bath

☐ 3-sleeping bags (5 lb. fill)
☐ 3-sponge pads
☐ 1-set of cooking utensils
☐ 1-tarp (cover game, etc.)
☐ 1-5 gal. water jug
☐ 1-shovel for latrine
☐ 1-large basin for dishes

Suggested Survival Kit:
☐ 1-space blanket
☐ 1-day food supply
    (dried food)
☐ 1-pack waterproof matches

☐ 1-20 ft. nylon rope
☐ 1-day liquid supply
    (2-8 oz. juice)
☐ 1-pack firestarter tabs

Rule Number One: Keep your footwear dry!

9

Physical Conditioning
For Elk Hunting

For Dr. Alden Glidden, a member of the North American Hunting Club from Oregon, hunting elk hasn't always been a winning—or even pleasant—proposition. Glidden first tried his hand—or more appropriately, his legs—at elk hunting in the early 1970s in Oregon's Wallowa Mountains. This range consists of numerous knife-back ridges. While hunting there you either hike straight up or straight down all day long, never on the level. It's typical elk hunting.

"At that time, I had just started my medical practice and had done nothing to stay in shape," Glidden recalls. "After the first day I was huffing and puffing and could hardly hunt. It was devastating."

Glidden doesn't take defeat lightly, so when he returned home he started jogging to get in shape for elk hunting.

"At first I would run, walk, run, walk for two miles," he said. "That got a little easier, so one day I ran a full three miles. After the run I threw up. That's how bad of shape I was in."

Glidden is an intense person who does things only one way—all out. He was so disgusted with his physical stature that he took up running seriously. As his running mileage increased, his weight gradually dropped from 160 pounds to 130, and soon he was running marathons.

Along with the weight loss, Glidden lost overall strength, so to supplement the running he now also lifts weights to strengthen his upper body and legs. With training he has doubled the amount of weight he can lift.

And it is to his off-season conditioning that Glidden credits his recent elk hunting successes in Idaho. He and his hunting partner, Irv Cater, who also runs to keep in shape for hunting, go into the Selway-Bitterroot Wilderness with an outfitter. Having learned the area, they now hunt on their own. Cater has taken bulls nearly every year for 20 straight years, and Glidden has not been blanked yet. He has taken bulls his first four consecutive years in Idaho. Both hunters contribute a good deal of their regular success to conditioning.

Condition As A Limiting Factor

That may be the key phrase in successful elk hunting. To succeed as a hunter you must systematically eliminate weaknesses that might limit your chances for bagging an animal. For a person who lives far from elk country, gaining knowledge of western game, or assembling the needed equipment, or transporting the horses, or learning how to camp, can be difficult. Really though, these shortcomings are no deterrent to successful hunting, because you can always hire an outfitter who has the needed hunting knowledge, equipment, horses and camp knowledge.

One thing no guide or outfitter can do, however, is to bring elk to you. He can't flatten out the topography and make the conditions any easier. He can't carry you on his back through the brush and set you in shooting position. He can't quiet your heaving lungs to help you place a careful shot. In short, he can't take the place of necessary physical conditioning. Even in outfitted hunting you must be able to get to the elk on your own and make your own shot. That's where physical conditioning comes in, and it's entirely your responsibility.

The Self-Guided Hunt

When hunting on your own, you shouldn't question the value of good conditioning. You must do all your own camp chores and meat packing, and chances are you'll be hunting on foot, so you'll be hiking long miles each day to find game. Over the years I've kept rough records of mileage hiked each day by myself and hunting partners. The average daily mileage falls between 8 and 10 miles—a short day entails five miles, and a long day 15—and most of this involves steep terrain. It's not unusual to climb a vertical distance of 2,500 feet.

On top of this you can throw in some high elevation. Most elk country lies at elevations higher than 5,000 feet, and in Colorado, you're lucky to find good country lower than 8,000 feet. Finally, add a few miles of blow-down timber that you have to climb over continually, and throw in some cold and wet weather that robs you of energy, and you might get a hint of the demands of elk hunting.

Because he was out of shape, NAHC member Dr. Alden Glidden's first elk hunting trips were painful experiences. Now he runs marathons and is more successful in his elk hunting.

Though horses save a lot of leg work, an outfitter can't flatten the terrain. You must be able to hike four to eight miles per day to reach good elk spots.

On a self-guided hunt you do all the work. Consider the long miles, the high altitudes and the heavy loads, and you'll quickly see the importance of being in shape.

Even when these realities are known, some hunters won't take them seriously. Not long ago a hunter from Florida called me to ask for information on hunting in Colorado. I suggested a mountain range near the town of Vail.

"But remember," I said, "that's terrible country and you have to be in shape. It's some of the most awful terrain I've ever seen."

"We're in great shape," the drawling voice on the phone assured me. "Me and my friends hike all the time and we run. We're in top condition. The country doesn't scare us."

"Well, okay," I said. "You know your ability. I just want to make it clear that those mountains aren't like anything you've ever seen in Florida. They're bad."

A couple of months later, in mid-September, my phone rang, and when I answered, a soft voice with a southern drawl greeted my ear. It was the man from Florida.

"We're down here in Kremmling, Colorado," he said. "We tried hunting where you suggested, but we can't hack it. We wondered if you could suggest a place for some flatlanders to find an elk?"

I don't relate that story to say, "I told you so." The point is only that you can easily underestimate the physical demands of elk hunting. Don't take it lightly.

Could you keep up with this man in the mountains? His name is Ron Dube and he's an outfitter in Buffalo, Wyoming. Dube says that 90 percent of his hunters are in poor physical condition, and as a result, many of them fail to kill game.

The Outfitted Hunt

Don't assume that warning applies only to hunting on your own. Most outfitters agree that poor condition, above all else, prevents most hunters from killing game.

"Poor physical condition definitely is a limiting factor in elk hunting," said Ron Dube, an outfitter in northeast Wyoming. "We take about 100 hunters a year, and I would say 90 of them are in too poor of shape to make the grade. They either can't get to the game in the first place, or by the time they do, they're so bushed they can't shoot straight.

"I want to make one thing clear," Dube said, "age has nothing to do with it. We've had 60-year-old guys here who could leave most 20-year-olds behind. It's a matter of training.

"I also don't think elevation is critical. The steepness and long miles are what gets to guys. It just wears them down. Each year a lot of trophy game gets away because sportsmen aren't in good enough shape."

Bruce Scott, an outfitter in Montana, echoed Dube's observations. When asked the major reason most hunters fail to collect game, Scott replied simply, "legs and lungs."

Your desired level of fitness, of course, depends on your goals. One outfitter told about three hunters who paid $2,000 apiece to hunt with him. They brought along a case of gin. All day they played cards and drank gin, and when the gin disappeared after five days—it was an eight-day hunt—they went home.

If that's your idea of a good hunt, fair enough, but if you sincerely plan to collect an animal, you'll have to condition something besides your elbows. The place to start, as Bruce Scott said, is your legs and lungs, and I'll add heart. *Physical conditioning is the most important step in successful elk hunting.*

Getting Started
Getting in shape can be dangerous to your health if you don't start right. Dr. Jill Upton, an exercise physiologist with Dr. Kenneth Cooper's Institute for Aerobic Research in Dallas, Texas, warned that any sedentary person over 35, and anyone, regardless of age, with a family history of heart disease, should undergo an electrocardiogram (ECG), a test that reveals weaknesses in the heart, before embarking on any kind of training program. More specifically, she recommends a stress ECG, which tests the heart after vigorous exercise that increases the person's heart rate to its maximum.

"A stress ECG will cost you $200 or so, but for anyone planning a strenuous hunt at high elevation, it's money well spent," Upton said. "It will help you plan a safe conditioning program, and it could save you from tragedy in the mountains."

Oxygen Consumption
A stress ECG also gives an excellent measure of general physical fitness. During a stress test doctors can measure your body's rate of oxygen consumption, which, physiologists say, is the most important gauge of overall condition. The better shape you're in the more efficiently your body can utilize oxygen.

Fat is another rough indicator of your physical condition. No direct

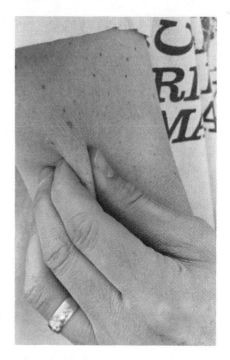

The pinch test gauges fitness. If you can pinch an inch or more on the back of your arm, you're probably overweight and in poor physical condition. This hunter can only grab about a ¼-inch. That's good!

correlation can be drawn between weight and physical condition, but a rough parallel does exist.

Fat has other implications for hunting other than as an indicator of poor condition. The fact is, fat is a burden in itself. It does no work, so it serves no more value in hiking than 20 pounds of rocks strapped to your back. Your body needs two percent body fat to function. Beyond that, fat is nothing but excess baggage. The average man, however has 23 percent body fat. The average women has 36 percent.

Getting In Shape

Okay. So you get an ECG and it tells you that your heart is all right but your ability to consume oxygen—that is, your physical condition—is terrible. What should you do? Embark on a conditioning program.

Steep-country, high elevation hunting—elk hunting—call for two kinds of conditioning: endurance and strength. Of the two, endurance—or as it's commonly called, aerobic training—is by far the more important. "Aerobic" means "with air," so aerobic training means conditioning with oxygen. Aerobic exercises are those you can sustain for long periods of time without building up an oxygen debt—walking, running, swimming, bicycling and so forth—opposed to anaerobic exercises, such as weight lifting or sprinting, during which you quickly build up an oxygen debt that forces you to stop and rest.

12-Minute Walking/Running Test
Distance (Miles) Covered in 12 Minutes

				Age (years)			
Fitness Category		13-19	20-29	30-39	40-49	50-59	60+
I. Very Poor	(men)	<1.30*	<1.22	<1.18	<1.14	<1.03	<.87
	(women)	<1.0	<.96	<.94	<.88	<.84	<.78
II. Poor	(men)	1.30-1.37	1.22-1.31	1.18-1.30	1.14-1.24	1.03-1.16	.87-1.02
	(women)	1.00-1.18	.96-1.11	.95-1.05	.88-.98	.84-.93	.78-.86
III. Fair	(men)	1.38-1.56	1.32-1.49	1.31-1.45	1.25-1.39	1.17-1.30	1.03-1.20
	(women)	1.19-1.29	1.12-1.22	1.06-1.18	.99-1.11	.94-1.05	.87-.98
IV. Good	(men)	1.57-1.72	1.50-1.64	1.46-1.56	1.40-1.53	1.31-1.44	1.21-1.32
	(women)	1.30-1.43	1.23-1.34	1.19-1.29	1.12-1.24	1.06-1.18	.99-1.09
V. Excellent	(men)	1.73-1.86	1.65-1.76	1.57-1.69	1.54-1.65	1.45-1.58	1.33-1.55
	(women)	1.44-1.51	1.35-1.45	1.30-1.39	1.25-1.34	1.19-1.30	1.10-1.18
VI. Superior	(men)	>1.87	>1.77	>1.70	>1.66	>1.59	>1.56
	(women)	>1.52	>1.46	>1.40	>1.35	>1.31	>1.19

*< Means "less than"; > means "more than."

1.5-Mile Run Test
Time (Minutes)

				Age (years)			
Fitness Category		13-19	20-29	30-39	40-49	50-59	60+
I: Very Poor	(men)	>15:31*	>16:01	>16:31	>17:31	>19:01	>20:01
	(women)	>18:31>	>19:01	>19:31	>20:01	>20:31	>21:01
II: Poor	(men)	12:11-15:30	14:01-16:00	14:44-16:30	15:36-17:30	17:01-19:00	19:01-20:00
	(women)	16:55-18:30	18:31-19:00	19:01-19:30	19:31-20:00	20:01-20:30	21:00-21:31
III: Fair	(men)	10:49-12:10	12:01-14:00	12:31-14:45	13:01-15:35	14:31-17:00	16:16-19:00
	(women)	14:31-16:54	15:55-18:30	16:31-19:00	17:31-19:30	19:01-20:00	19:31-20:30
IV: Good	(men)	9:41-10:48	10:46-12:00	11:01-12:30	11:31-13:00	12:31-14:30	14:00-16:15
	(women)	12:30-14:30	13:31-15:54	14:31-16:30	15:56-17:30	16:31-19:00	17:31-19:30
V: Excellent	(men)	8:37-9:40	9:45-10:45	10:00-11:00	10:30-11:30	11:00-12:30	11:15-13:59
	(women)	11:50-12:29	12:30-13:30	13:00-14:30	13:45-15:55	14:30-16:30	16:30-17:30
VI: Superior	(men)	<8:37	<9:45	<10:00	<10:30	<11:00	<11:15
	(women)	<1:50	<12:30	<13:00	<13:45	<14:30	<16:30

*< Means "less than"; > means "more than."

Taken from: *The Aerobics Program for Total Well Being*, by Dr. Kenneth Cooper M. Evans and Company, Inc., New York.

First, you might ask, why is endurance training so important? In a nutshell, it strengthens and conditions all systems of your body.

A Strong Heart

Perhaps most important, aerobic training enlarges and strengthens your heart. A well-conditioned heart pumps more blood with each squeeze than a weak heart does, so it can do more work with less effort. That's often reflected in a slower pulse rate. Dr. Upton said the average person has a resting pulse rate of about 72 beats per minute, but with training that normally drops to 60 or slower. Many athletes have resting pulse rates slower than 40 beats per minute. I can see the effects of training on my own heart rate. At one time my resting pulse rate was 60 beats per minute. After several years of running and other aerobic training, it has dropped to 47 beats per minute.

Not only does a strong heart beat slower at rest than a weak heart, but it can sustain a higher level of exertion for longer periods of time, and it recovers from exertion much more quickly. During a hard hike, your heart rate might climb to 160 beats per minute or higher. If you're in good shape, you probably can sustain that level of performance for an hour or more to keep right on your guide's heels. Just as significantly, when you do stop to rest, your pulse will drop to a normal rate quickly. Conceivably, if you're in shape, it will drop from 160 to 90 beats a minute or slower within five minutes, which means you'll feel rested and raring to go after a short breather.

In contrast, if you're in poor shape, you won't be able to maintain a heart rate of 160 beats per minute for more than a few minutes, which means your guide will continually have to stop and wait for you. And even worse, after five minutes' rest your heart may still be thudding away at 120 beats per minute or faster, and you'll be lying on the ground puffing as your guide says, "Come on, let's go or we'll never reach those elk."

Other Benefits

Aerobic training brings about many other physiological changes. It increases the volume of blood in your body and increases the number of capillaries to the muscles so that the muscles are more efficiently served by the blood. It also expands lung capacity, so that your lungs can efficiently enrich the blood with fresh oxygen and remove carbon dioxide and other wastes.

Aerobic training also burns up fat and replaces it with lean muscle. Dieting is one way to lose weight, but most physiologists agree that dieting without exercise is self defeating. To effectively reduce the percentage of body fat, you must apply some form of endurance training. Aerobic training, in short, makes your body a leaner, meaner machine.

Fatigue is the inevitable byproduct of prolonged exertion, and you must expect to feel some in elk hunting. But being in good shape will minimize its effects.

Fatigue

It's one thing to hunt hard one day, and it's another to hunt hard for eight days straight. Fatigue is defined as "the inability to maintain a given exercise intensity." Fatigue accompanies all hard hunting. It's caused by a depletion of the body's stored energy and a buildup of waste products in muscles. Rest is essential to reverse these effects, but on any western hunt, you'll hunt long days and get little rest, and gradually you'll experience fatigue.

That's inevitable, but the better shape you're in to start with, the longer you can delay it. A finely tuned body, like finely tuned engine, burns incoming fuel—food and oxygen—and eliminates waste products—carbon dioxide and others—efficiently, and fatigue will be much less of a problem than for the poorly tuned body.

Altitude

Aerobic training also addresses that one final obstacle in western hunting—altitude. By training at sea level you can't prepare for all high-elevation problems, but again, the more efficient your body, the better it can deal with thin, high-altitude air.

We all have a certain aerobic capacity at sea level, and the better your condition, the higher that capacity. If you're in poor shape it might be 25, and in good shape, 50. Dr. Barbara Drinkwater, an authority on altitude physiology, said you can go up to about 5,000 feet elevation with litte change in that capacity, but from there on up, it declines steadily. From 7,000 to 10,000 feet elevation, Drinkwater said, you lose 10 to 15 percent of maximum aerobic capacity. In other words if you have a sea-level capacity of 50, it would drop to 45 at 7,000 feet. That happens even in the best-conditioned athlete, but obviously the greater your capacity to begin with, the higher it will remain at altitude, and that's one major benefit of aerobic training for western hunting.

Safety

One final aspect of aerobic benefit can't be ignored, and that's health safety. In short, good physical condition lowers the potential for heart attack and stroke.

One risk factor directly related to heart attack is cholesterol level. Research shows that regular exercise reduces cholesterol levels and lowers blood pressure, thus directly reducing the potential for heart problems. it has also been found that exercise helps many people quit smoking, so a regular training program significantly reduces the three major coronary risk factors.

Running is one of the best forms of aerobic exercise. For any activity to benefit your heart and lungs, you must maintain your training heart rate for at least 20 minutes, three times per week.

The Aerobic Training Program

Heart Rate

Three variables govern the value of aerobic training: oxygen consumption, duration and frequency. You would need expensive equipment to measure oxygen consumption, but you can roughly gauge it in terms of heart (pulse) rate. Most physiologists use a set formula to define maximum heart rate: 220 minus age. Thus, if you're 20 years old, your maximum heart rate is about 200 beats per minute (220-20 (your age) ^{5} 200. If you're 40, it's 180).

Luke Klaja, a member of the 1980 Olympic weight lifting team, and also a physical therapist and althletic trainer, said you must train at a given heart rate to improve physical fitness. A person in very poor condition should train at 70 percent of maximum heart rate, a person in good shape at 80 percent, and a well-trained athlete at 85 percent. Here's the formula:

220 - age = maximum heart rate x .70 (.80 or .85) = training heart rate.

Thus, if you're 40 years old and in poor shape, you should begin training at 70 percent of 180, or about 126 heart beats per minute (220 - 40 = 180 x .70 = 126). If you're 40 and in good shape, you would train at 80 percent of 180, or 144 per minute.

To monitor your pulse, exercise long enough to raise your heart rate, and then stop and take your pulse for six seconds. Multiply by 10 to get the beats per minute. (You don't want to count for longer than six seconds because your heart will begin to slow down and give you an inaccurate count). If the rate is slower than the prescribed training rate, exercise harder; if it's too high, slow down.

The beauty of this system is that it's self-regulating. If you're in poor shape, a slow walk might bring your pulse up to the training rate, but after a few weeks of training, you may have to jog or run to hit the perscribed rate.

If you're just starting out on an exercise program, you're wise to monitor your heart rate carefully and to limit your activity to the prescribed bounds outlined above. The person who trains regularly, however, probably won't go to that trouble. After awhile, you learn to read your body, and you'll instinctively regulate your pace. One good rule of thumb is the "talk test." Set a pace at which you can carry on a converstation. If you're puffing so hard you can't talk, you're probably pushing yourself too hard.

Duration

Physiologists have found that activity must be sustained for a given length of time to be of benefit. Few agree on the exact duration, but 15 minutes seems to be a reasonable minimum. If you exercise with your heart rate at the training level for 15 minutes, you improve fitness. If you do it for less time, you don't improve. For maximum benefit your heart must sustain the training rate. That's why stop and go sports like handball or tennis, which allow your heart to rest periodically, don't improve fitness as quickly as continuous sports like walking, running and swimming. Choose one of these activities and do it continuously for a minimum of 15 minutes.

Frequency

Most physiologists agree that you must train on three, non-consecutive days a week to maintain a given level of conditioning, and you must train four days or more to improve. If you allow more than two days between sessions, you lose conditioning. That's why it's important to spread out your training. If you train three straight days and rest four, you'll lose some of the benefit during the rest days that you gained on the training days.

To avoid injury and fatigue, work up gradually. You can't get in shape in a week, so start out at the prescribed heart rate and stick with it.

If you're in poor shape, train at a slow pace for 15 minutes, three times a day. As your condition improves, switch to longer periods. A well-conditioned person will get more benefit out of a 45-minute session once a day.

Recommended Aerobic Training Program

Athletic trainer Luke Klaja recommends the following program to condition for mountain hunting. Remember, to be of value, aerobic workouts must last a minimum of 15 minutes at your training heart rate, and you must work out at least three or more times a week.

Begin by walking. Walk for 10 minutes at a stiff pace, and increase that two to three minutes per week until you're up to 30 to 40 minutes a day. Keep you pulse rate within the appropriate range:

220 - age = maximum heart rate x .70 (poor shape) = training rate
x .80 (average shape)
x .85 (excellent shape)

From that starting point, increase time and heart rate, which means, after your fitness level improves, you must gradually increase your pace. After two months you may have to jog or run to attain the same heart rate you got by slow walking at first. That's good because it means you're getting in shape. It doesn't matter what kind of exercise you do as long as you sustain your heart rate for a long period of time. The best aerobic exercises—walking, hiking, jogging, swimming, bicycling, rope skipping, calisthenics—utilize large muscles. If you get bored doing just one of these, alternate them. You can swim one day and run the next, or swim during the week and bicycle on weekends.

The Institute for Aerobic Research has found that you must sustain an aerobic exercise for at least 20 minutes four times a week, or for at least 30 minutes three times a week to maintain an adequate basic level of fitness. Remember, however, that that produces only basic fitness. It improves your capacity for exertion and reduces coronary risk, and certainly it's enough to improve your ability to hunt without undue fatigue.

However, it may not be enough to sustain you through days of hard hunting. Mountain hunting can force you into levels of endurance you never reach in a fundamental aerobics training program. It's impossible to relate the demands of any training program directly to the rigors of mountain hunting. The question always remains: How much training is enough?

While a minimum fitness training program may be adequate to help you hunt comfortably with an outfitter who provides horses, or to hunt by vehicle, it may not prepare you for a self-guided backcountry hunt where you must walk many miles and do all of your own packing. For that kind of hunt, I think training should involve a half-hour to an hour of aerobic activity, at least five times a week.

Strength Training

Endurance training may be more important for mountain hunting, but strength training can enhance your hunt, too. As physiologist Covert Bailey said: "Muscle is like a car engine. For mountain driving you need a big engine to pull heavy loads up steep grades, and you need strong muscles for the same reason."

Virtually all western mountains have slopes of 15 to 40 percent, and many exceed 70 percent. The average stairway is about 70 percent. As you know, it takes a lot more strength and energy to hike stairs than to walk a sidewalk, so if you picture yourself climbing those stairs all day long, you get an inkling of what western hunting is like. The stronger your legs are, the less energy required to hike a given distance.

Also, few aerobic activities strengthen the upper body. In putting up tents, lifting heavy packs, wrestling elk meat and any of the other myriad heavy chores that go hand in hand with elk hunting, you need generally good muscle tone throughout your body.

Strengthening The Legs

Olympian Luke Klaja said that strength for hiking comes from four big muscle groups in the legs: quadraceps (front of thighs); hamstrings (back of thighs); buttocks; and calves. He recommends three major exercises to strengthen these muscles. These can be done at home without weights, but Klaja recommends doing them with weights because you increase strength and endurance much faster with them.

Most of these exercises can be done with free weights (barbells) or with machines such as the Universal Gym. Klaja said you'll make faster progress with free weights because they make greater demands on your muscles, but machines give you better control so injury is less likely.

Start out with one set of 10 to 12 repetitions. Weight should be heavy enough so you have to work aggressively to complete the final repetition. After your third workout, do two sets of each exercise, and after your eighth workout increase it to three sets of 10 to 12 repetitions. Do all three sets of one exercise—with about 60 seconds rest between each set—before going on to the next exercise. This helps build endurance as well as strength.

1. SQUATS: These build primarily the quadraceps and buttocks. Stand straight with the weight on your shoulders, squat as far as possible and stand back up. It's important you keep your back straight and not to bounce at the bottom.

2. LUNGES: These build the hamstrings and buttocks. Stand straight with the weight on your shoulders. Lunge straight ahead with your left foot as far as possible and bend your left knee, keeping your right knee as straight as possible. Thrust with your left leg to push yourself back to the standing position. Repeat by lunging forward with your right leg and pushing back with your left. Remember to keep your back straight.

3. CALF RAISES: Stand with your toes raised three to four inches on a block of wood and your heels on the floor. Support the weight on your shoulders. Rise on your tip toes and ease back down. Repeat.

Strengthening The Upper Body

Upper body strength is also important when elk hunting. Here are exercises you can do at home without weights.

1. PUSH UP: Lie face down on the floor, the palms of your hands flat on the floor beside your shoulders. Keeping your back straight, push yourself up until your arms are straight, and then let yourself back to the floor. Repeat.

2. PULL UP-PALMS OUT: Hang by your hands from a bar with

There are other aerobic exercises besides running, swimming and cycling. Here Dr. Alden Glidden uses a Nordic ski machine which simulates the motions of cross-country skiing.

Lunges strengthen the hamstrings and the buttocks. They can be done with or without weights.

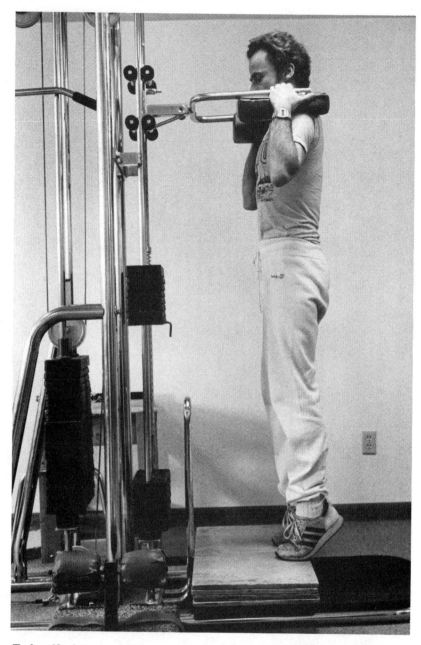

To do calf raises, stand with your toes raised about three inches on a block of wood. Then rise on your toes as far as possible, then lower back down. Here Al Glidden does them on a Universal Gym. The amount of weight can be varied.

Situps strengthen the torso and prevent back injuries. As Glidden does here, always do situps with knees bent to get the most benefit and prevent injury.

The benchpress develops sheer strength in the arms and upper body. Important for lifting and toting required in elk hunting.

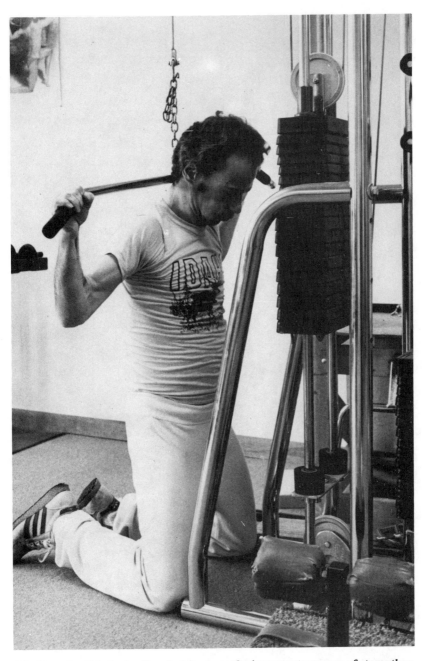

The lateral pull is demanding, but it serves the important purpose of strengthening shoulders and arms for a pack trip.

As directed by a trainer or complete fitness texts, you can add exercises to specifically train segments of your body that may be especially lacking.

your palms facing away from your body. Pull yourself up to the bar and ease back down. Repeat. Do as many as you can comfortably.

3. PULL UP-PALMS IN: Hang from the bar with your palms facing towards you and pull up until your chin touches the bar. Ease back down. Repeat. Do as many as you can comfortably.

4. BENT KNEE SIT UP: Lie on your back with your knees bent and your hands locked behind your head. Sit upright and then let yourself back down. Repeat.

5. BACK EXTENSION: Lie face down on the floor with a pillow under your stomach and your arms at your sides. Arch your back, lifting your head as high as possible, and pinch your shoulder blades together. Repeat.

Exercises Done With Weights

1. BENCH PRESS: This can be done with free weights or a Universal Gym. Lie on your back and hold the weight at arm's length. Lower the bar to your chest and push it back up. The weight should be light enough so you can complete 12 repetitions. The last rep should be a challenge but not death.

2. SHOULDER PRESS: While sitting, hold the bar at chest level and lift it overhead to arm's length, then lower it to chest level again. Again, start with weight you can handle easily enough to complete 10 to 12 repetitions.

3. ARM CURL: Hold the bar in your hands with the palms up. Hold your elbows tight to your body and curl the bar to your chest. Let it back down until your arms are fully extended. Repeat. Work up to three sets of 10 to 12 reps.

4. LATERAL PULLDOWN: This exercise is done on the Universal Gym. You hold onto the bar overhead, which is attached to the weights by means of pulleys, and pull the bar down to your shoulders and slowly let it back up. Repeat. Work up to three sets of 10 to 12 reps.

Specificity Training

One other training philosophy warrants mention, and it's what physiologists call "specificity training."

"Ideally you should train specifically for what you plan to do," says Dr. Barbara Drinkwater, an exercise physiologist at the University of Washington. "To train for mountain hiking, you want to hike. Find some steep hills (or stairways if you live in flat country—author). Start light, wearing your hiking boots but no pack, and climb at a pace you can maintain for 45 minutes or so. When that gets comfortable, carry 20 pounds in a pack and gradually work up to 65 pounds. When you've hit a maximum weight, increase your hiking speed."

This kind of training not only strengthens the legs, but it builds your aerobic capacity, and it works on other systems of the body that you'll use in hunting. I've used this approach several different years. I continue my running program, but for about a month before the hunting season, I forego running at least two days a week and replace it with hiking. I start with a 20-pound pack and gradually work up to 70 pounds, which is about the maximum I can handle.

I've found several benefits, in addition to the aerobic and strength benefits. First, carrying the pack gets my muscles used to packing so I avoid sore, stiff shoulders and back during the first few days of my hunt. Second, by carrying a pack under field conditions, I learn to gauge my ability in terms of hiking speed and the amount of weight I can handle. That eliminates a lot of unpleasant surprises when I start hunting.

Third, it conditions me for the up-and-down nature of hunting. Perhaps more damaging than any other aspect of mountain hunting is the steep grades and the strain they place on joints, tendons and muscles. Hiking downhill under a heavy load particularly strains the knees. By hiking for a few weeks before the season you can condition for this kind of stress and avoid some real pain while you're hunting. One year a friend and I drove to the top of a high ridge and backpacked a couple of miles straight down to a canyon bottom. I had been backpacking near home to condition for this hunt, but my friend had only been running. Aerobically he was in great shape, but he wasn't conditioned to steep grades and heavy loads. I hiked down comfortably, but halfway to the bottom, my friend's knees were on fire with pain, and he had to stop every 100 yards or so to rest them. Needless to say, my hunt got off to a more pleasant start than his, and specific conditioning for mountain conditions deserves the credit.

In The End

Conditioning may not be the total answer to elk hunting success, but it can play a big part. It will help eliminate two major limiting factors—exhaustion and fatigue. You have to carefully select your gear, choose a competent outfitter, hunt a good area and perfect your shooting, but all of these mean nothing if you're too exhausted to hunt. Start with good physical condition and other things will fall into place.

10

After Your Elk Is Down

If, after coming from a deer hunting background, you've found elk hunting comparatively tough, wait until you get a bull on the ground. That's where you'll really find out the difference between deer and elk. You'll first notice the difference when you try to roll the animal over for gutting; it will become painfully obvious when you start packing out the meat.

Time-worn advice says to get your animal to a cooler as soon as possible. That's well and good, and if you're camped next to a road near town, and you down an animal where you can drive to it, you probably can pull it off. That kind of access solves a lot of problems. You can use the winch on your vehicle to hang parts of the animal, or even the whole animal, in a tree for skinning. And you can get the meat to a locker for immediate cooling.

But what if you're five miles back in the boonies with nothing but a packframe and two legs for transportation? That puts a new light on the subject, and obviously under those conditions getting meat to a cooler quickly is impossible. To complicate things further, many elk hunts take place in August and September during warm weather. In some cases, you may have to leave meat in the woods for a week or more before you can get it to cold storage.

Even under the worst conditions, however, there is no excuse for losing meat. Many butchers who handle wild game can tell horror stories that would turn a buzzard's stomach, and in most cases, the meat has spoiled only because of carelessness or ignorance on the part of the hunters.

Go Prepared

First comes quick recovery of animals. That can be a problem for all hunters, but it's a special consideration for bow hunters because elk may travel some distance, even after a vital hit, and recovery may take some time.

Clem Stechelin, a commercial meat cutter in Springfield, Oregon, said that during the 1983 archery season, hunters brought in three elk that were partially or totally soured.

Why had this happened? The animals had lain in the field overnight. With their heavy bodies and thick hides, elk do not cool well, even in cold weather, and you can just about assume that an elk recovered the day after the shot will be spoiled. *But that's no excuse to give up looking!* I have recovered bull elk that have lain dead in the field overnight, and the meat has been fine. Never give up on the basis of assumption.

It's important to prepare before you ever go into the field, and that means having the needed items to locate and butcher an animal. Perhaps most important is a good flashlight. If you hit an animal in late afternoon, you may have to trail into the night. If you have to go back to camp to get a light, you lose much valuable time. A good light should be part of your survival gear anyway, but it serves double duty in helping find game, and you can easily follow a blood trail in the beam of a flashlight. Carry spare batteries and bulb to make sure you don't lose your light source when you need it most.

Survival gear such as a reliable fire starter, map and compass, and emergency shelter also play a part in recovering animals. If you're afraid of getting caught out overnight, you may give up the trail prematurely and return to camp. But if you're prepared to find your way back to camp in the dark (flashlight, map, compass) or to stay overnight in the field (fire and emergency shelter), you'll fearlessly stick right with that trail until you find your animal. It could mean the difference between saving and losing the meat.

Other gear items are essential, too. The need for a good knife for gutting and skinning is obvious, but just as important is a small steel or stone for resharpening the knife as you work on an elk. Always carry 50 feet or so of cord, especially if you hunt alone. You can use it to tie the elk's legs out of the way as you work, and you may need it to hang meat in a tree. In warm weather when you must skin an elk immediately, it's also important to carry lightweight game bags to protect the meat from flies and dirt. A folding saw comes in handy for cutting

Get meat to the cooler as quickly as possible! But in practice it's going to take these hunters a while to do so. That's why it is important for all elk hunters to have special knowledge of meat care.

The bare essentials for field care of meat include: flashlight, 50 feet of nylon cord, knife, sharpening steel, saw and game bags. You might want to add a pocketsize block and tackle.

bones, and one addition I plan to carry from now on is a small block-and-tackle. Some versions are small enough to slip into a pocket, and they weigh only a few ounces. Trying to hang meat out of bear reach (most elk country has bears) can break your back, so a small hoist could prevent a lot of strain.

The Way Of All Flesh

Meat spoils in two ways—from the inside out and from the outside in. Of most immediate concern is internal spoilage, or bone sour. Bob Dixon, a butcher at the Oregon State University meat science lab, explains that when an animal dies, its organs stop working but its muscle cells don't. They go right on doing their jobs, and in the process they create heat. In a live animal, circulating blood performs the same function as water in a car's cooling system—it carries away excess heat to maintain a constant body temperature, about 101 degrees in the case of big game. After an animal dies the cells keep producing heat, but with a kaput cooling system, body temperature rises to 110 degrees or higher. Unless this heat is dissipated, the meat will sour.

All meat contains bacteria. In live animals natural mechanisms keep these bacteria under control, but when an animal dies the bacteria can run rampant. They grow best in temperatures from 60 to 100 degrees. If an animal is cooled to eliminate all body heat within 24 hours, bacteria cannot grow and bone sour isn't a concern. But if cooling is slow, bacteria

An elastic band will hold a flashlight on your head for skinning and caping after dark.

run wild, and the result is souring that spreads quickly through the meat. Souring is a function of temperature, not location, but meat normally sours first in the shoulders and hip sockets because these thick points retain body heat longer than less-meaty areas.

Even well-cooled meat can spoil from the outside in. Bacteria and mold are always present in soil and water, and they breed rapidly on meat to produce slime and mold. The organisms grow even under refrigeration, so there's a limit to how long you can hang meat even in cold weather, but the warmer the air the faster they grow and the faster meat will spoil. The major defense against external spoilage is to keep meat cool, clean and dry.

Field Dressing

Meat preservation starts with proper field dressing. Under standard field-dressing procedures, you will slit the hide from the animal's anus up to the brisket, taking care not to puncture the stomach or intestines. Cut the skin around both sides of the penis and testicles (if it's a bull) and lay these organs back between the legs out of the way. Don't cut the penis or you'll squirt urine everywhere. Cut cleanly around the anus to free the large intenstine from the hide. On a cow, cut around the anus and vaginal opening so that these are freed completely from the hide.

Now reach inside and start pulling innards out through the slit in the belly. You'll have to reach well up inside to cut the diaphragm away from the rib cage and the wind pipe and esophagus at the base of the neck. Be careful with these maneuvers or you might find one of your fingers among the lungs and other offal. That's a sobering thought when you're a few miles from the nearest help. If you stop to think that one slip with that knife into an artery could mean you'll die right there, you'll cut slowly and deliberately.

As you cut things loose, keep rolling innards from the body cavity onto the ground. Pull gently on the intestines to pull the anus and attached penis (or vagina) out through the body cavity. You may have to slip your knife alongside the anus and around inside the pelvis to free organs there. As you do, be careful not to cut the urine bladder or you'll end up with a real mess. When you've pretty well cored around the inside of the pelvis with your knife, you can pull the big intestine with the anus attached out through the body cavity.

After you've removed all organs, slit the skin on forward over the brisket (chest) to the chin (unless you plan to cape the animal for mounting, which will be covered later). Remove the entire wind pipe and esophagus, and split the brisket with a saw or hatchet so the animal can be opened to cool.

Your procedure from that point on will depend greatly on conditions. You'll have to decide whether to wash the carcass; whether to skin the animal or leave the hide on; whether to cape it; whether to quarter it, leave it whole, or bone it, and so forth.

To Wash Or Not To Wash

One myth related to meat handling says you should never put water on a carcass. Indeed there are good reasons not to. Water contains meat-spoiling bacteria, so washing can contaminate meat, and moisture also promotes growth of bacteria so the drier you can keep the carcass, the better. If you've shot an animal in the neck or head, and the body cavity is clean, simply use a cloth to wipe any blood or dirt and call it done.

On the other hand, gun-shot wounds, particularly in the body, can contaminate meat badly and washing may be the only alternative. Water in itself doesn't affect meat. After all, the body cavity is already wet so a little more water won't hurt; meat processing plants thoroughly wash and scrub every animal. One year I killed an elk, and because of the nature of the hit, the body cavity was a mess and badly needed washing. We couldn't get water to the animal, so a friend and I quartered it and scrubbed the quarters in a nearby stream. That was one of the cleanest animals I've ever killed, and it was one of the finest eating even though we kept it in the backcountry for several days after the washing. Cold water not only cleans dirty meat but helps to cool it fast.

However, don't wash meat *after* it has cooled. Bacteria and mold already have taken hold by then, and water will only aggravate the problem. After you've washed an animal, hang the meat to dry. Bacteria grow most rapidly in moisture, so once the animal is clean and dry, take great pains to keep it that way, which includes wrapping it with clean game bags and getting it under cover during rain or snow.

To Skin Or Not To Skin

One hotly debated subject is skinning. Many hunters say: "You must skin an animal immediately. Getting that hide off is the most important thing!"

In some cases that's true. Professor Ray Field, an authority on meat care at the University of Wyoming, said:

"If the temperature is 70 degrees during the day, and there's no frost at night, then you had better get that hide off immediately so the animal will cool fast." Field's research showed, for example, that the thickest part of a skinned deer leg dropped to air temperature (38 degrees) in 10 hours, but a hide-on leg required 14 hours. Slow cooling, as pointed out earlier, is a major reason for bone sour. In any warm weather, which includes virtually all hunting during the September rut, plan to skin out your animal on the spot if you can't get it to cold storage facilities within a day.

Unfortunately, skinning has its drawbacks. For one thing, it opens up meat to dirt and flies. To cope with those problems during early seasons, always carry lightweight, cheesecloth game bags, and as you skin and quarter an animal, immediately slip the meat into bags to keep it clean. Game bags must be light enough to allow good air circulation but tightly woven enough to prevent flies from blowing their eggs through the cloth. *Never* put freshly skinned meat in plastic bags because plastic prevents rapid cooling.

When you skin an animal in the field, leave the heavy layers of fat in place. Fat protects the meat from dirt and prevents drying. However, all fat should be trimmed off before you cut and wrap the meat.

Don't take for granted that just because you skin an elk it will cool well. Rich LaRocco shot a bull elk one evening in Colorado, and we had skinned, quartered and laid it out on rocks to cool by midnight. The next morning a quarter-inch of ice coated every puddle of water. We felt good because the meat would be cold, but we discovered there were very warm areas next to the hip sockets. We opened up the hams

During cold weather, it may be wisest to leave the hide on an elk. It keeps the meat clean and moist. Note these hunters splitting the hind quarters with the hide on!

to cool and the meat was fine, but that experience made us aware of body-heat problems in heavy animals.

Bob Vierling, a federal meat inspector, said that bone sour can be a problem even on domestic cattle that are skinned and hung in coolers at 34 degrees. On massive domestic bulls, Vierling said, butchers separate muscles on the inside of the hind legs down to the bone, and they slit under the shoulder blades and pull back the front legs so air can circulate there. This same procedure on elk in the field assures overnight cooling right to the bone.

Ray Field believes the only justification for skinning an animal is to speed up cooling during warm weather. Otherwise, he strongly advocates leaving the hide on.

"The hide keeps out dirt, hair, water—the things that introduce bacteria and spoil meat," Field said. "Meat under the hide is virtually sterile, so spoilage is much less likely in unskinned animals. Hide also keeps meat from drying out so you don't have to do a lot of trimming."

Field recommends leaving the hide on even in warm weather if the animal can be taken to a cooler and skinned there the day of the kill. And he recommends leaving the hide on in the field—until you butcher the animal—if there's frost at night so the carcass can be cooled quickly. Once the meat is thoroughly cooled you don't have to worry about bone sour, and not only does the hide keep meat clean but the insulation it provides keeps meat cool during the day.

Incidentally, studies show that hide left on meat does not affect flavor. Researchers at the University of Wyoming halved several deer, elk and antelope. They skinned one half of each animal and left hide on the other, and they aged these halves for several days. When they cut up the meat and cooked roasts from each side, trained tasters could not tell which cuts came from the skinned sides and which came from the skin-on sides.

Caping An Elk

If you plan to have the head of your elk mounted, you'll need to cape it rather than skinning the whole animal. Incidentally, even if you don't plan to have it mounted, you can sell good elk capes to taxidermists for enough to pay for part of your hunting trip. Most of the following suggestions were offered by taxidermist Ralph Vaden of Klamath Falls, Oregon.

First, make sure you leave plenty of hide for the taxidermist to work with. Start your cut behind the front shoulder hump, and slit the hide straight down the chest, staying behind the front leg. Now cut from that slit along the backbone right up the back of the neck to about the middle of the ears. Never cut the under side of the neck on a cape you plan

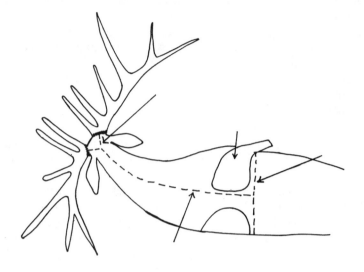

to have mounted. From the point at the middle of the ears, cut the hide diagonally to the base of each antler. This will produce a V-shaped cut on the back of the head. Next, skin out the neck right to the base of the head, being careful not to cut the hide. Try to leave all meat on the carcass. You can now cut the head off where it attaches to the neck.

If you can get to a taxidermist that same day, you can leave the head and cape in one piece and take the whole thing to the taxidermist for skinning. However, if you have to spend several more days in the field, you're wise to skin out the head to prevent spoilage of the hide.

Cut the ears loose from the head, cutting as close to the head as possible, and then work the hide off the antler bases. The hide is very tight here, and you'll probably cut it to shreds if you try to skin it off with a knife, so use a blunt object like a screw driver and pry the hide loose from the antlers.

When you get to the eyes, be very careful not to cut the eyelids. You can slip your finger into the eye socket and pull the lid out to avoid cutting it. On the nose leave a fairly thick piece of cartilage on the hide, and cut the lips off well back into the inside of the mouth to give the taxidermist plenty to work with. Now cut the antlers off the skull with a saw or ax. Make your cut through the eye sockets and well down the nose so the taxidermist has some bone to work with.

You can handle a cape pretty much as you would handle meat. Spread

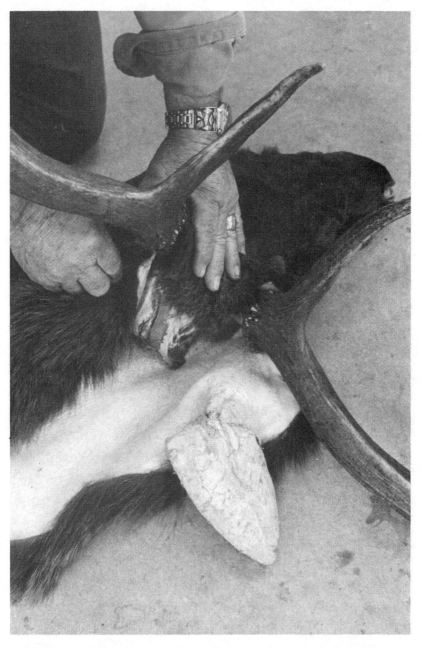

Hide has been slit up the back of the neck to the ears and cut diagonally to the base of the antlers. The "V" shaped flap of skin fits back over the skull. (For demonstration purposes, this is a tanned cape with ears turned inside out.)

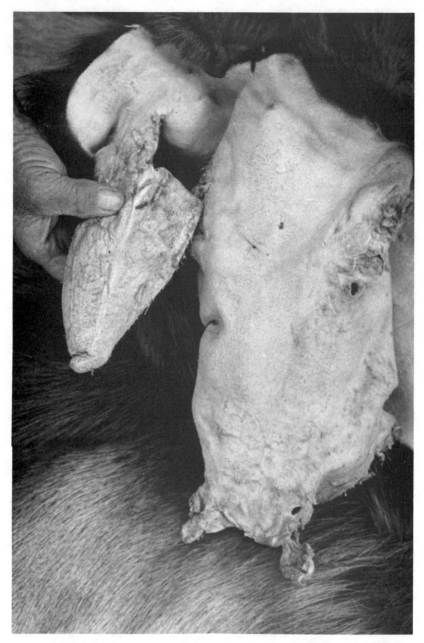

For keeping over several days, you must turn the ears for salting. This is a tanned cape with the ears and head turned. Note that the hide is cut well up inside the nostrils.

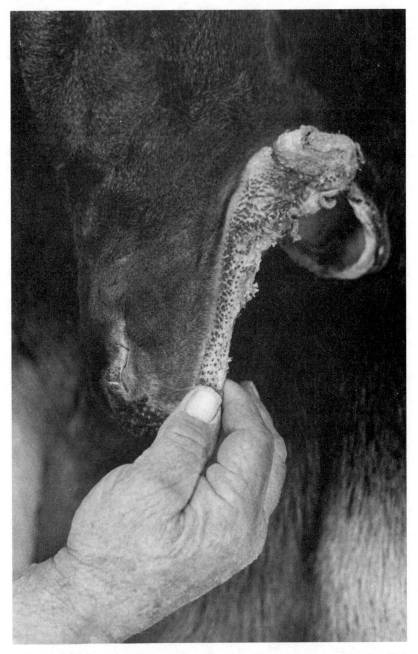

Cut well back into the mouth to give the taxidermist something to work with. This photo shows the lips on a tanned cape.

To remove the antlers, cut the skull through the eye sockets and down the nose to give the taxidermist plenty of bone to work with.

it out so that air circulates around it to cool the hide quickly, and then hang it in a cool, shaded place, out of the sun. You can keep it this way for at least a week if the weather is cool.

In warm weather, or if you'll be in camp longer than a week, you should salt the cape. Before you salt it you must turn the ears to remove the cartilage. If you salt it without turning the ears, the salt will draw out so much moisture the ears can't be turned later. With a blunt stick or wedge of some kind, begin breaking the hide away from the cartilage on the inside of the ear. Once you've got it started, you probably can slip your finger between the hide and cartilage to separate them, and then you'll be able to turn the ear inside out. Do this to both ears before you salt the cape. To salt an elk cape adequately, you need about five pounds of salt. Make sure you work the salt especially well into the lips, nose, eyes, and ears. Roll the hide and keep it out of the sun.

Reducing An Elk To Size

In some cases you may be able to field dress an elk, load the animal whole into your pickup, and take it back to camp or to a commercial locker for skinning and butchering. If that's the case, all the more power to you.

But if the animal must be left in the field for any time at all—say overnight—you must reduce it to smaller pieces to promote cooling. At the very least, it must be split down the center of the backbone. You can split an animal with a small saw, but it's hard work. My friend Roger Iveson recommends using two hatchets. Starting at the neck (the head has been cut off at the base of the skull) Iveson lays the sharp blade of one hatchet against the bone, and then he hammers it through with the other hatchet. You can split a bull elk from head to tail fairly quickly that way. You also can chop an elk in two lengthwise with a single ax, but it takes good aim and isn't as neat as the two-hatchet method.

In many cases you'll want to reduce it to smaller pieces yet, especially if you're alone. Few hunters are strong enough to handle half an elk, so you'll want to reduce the elk to at least quarters to make handling it easier. Also, if you plan to have a packer haul it out with horses, you'll want to quarter it. Most packers prefer to have elk split into fairly even quarters.

To quarter an elk, split it down the middle as described above. Or you might find it easier to cut the animal crosswise first before splitting it lengthwise. To get the quarters as even in weight as possible, many packers like to make the crosswise split just in front of the third rib. That is, starting with the farthest rib back, count forward three and cut between the ribs, leaving the back three ribs on the hind quarters. After

Most horse packers like to have an elk cut into evenly weighted quarters to make a balanced load on their pack animals.

you've sliced the ribs cleanly apart all the way to the backbone, cut the backbone in half. You can use a saw or ax, or if a couple of you are working on it, you can twist the backbone in half, and then simply cut the meat with a knife to free the back halves from the front.

You can quarter an elk this way either with the hide on or off. If you've skinned the animal, slip each quarter into a clean game bag as soon as you remove it from the animal.

After splitting or quartering an elk, either hang or lay the pieces on rocks or logs to ensure good air circulation. In Ray Field's studies, the temperature of meat lying next to the ground or on a truck bed generally was three to eight degrees warmer than it was for meat with good air circulation. Hanging heavy meat is about the most backbreaking job known to man, so one good addition to your elk hunting gear is a small block and tackle.

To Bone Or Not To Bone

Boning is the process of removing all bones from the meat, or as is more often the case in the field, removing all meat from the bones.

Again, boning has its proponents and opponents, and the choice of whether to bone depends on the circumstances.

First, why should you *not* bone out an elk? The less meat you expose to the elements, the less chance for spoilage, and boning opens up meat to dirt and contamination. By exposing a large amount of meat to the air, it also promotes excessive drying, so that you'll have to trim and discard more meat during the butchering process. As a general rule, you should bone an animal only as a last resort when benefits outweigh the drawbacks.

In many cases they do, however, so I consider boning a "must know" technique, especially for backcountry elk hunting. One major benefit is to reduce weight for packing. If you plan to backpack your own meat, there's absolutely no sense in carrying an ounce more than you have to. By boning out an animal, you carry only pure edible meat, and leave all the bones and scraps in the woods.

Boning also allows rapid dissipation of body heat, which may help save some animals. In 1983 I shot an elk late one afternoon, and we didn't find it until the next morning. Elk generally sour if they lay overnight, so needless to say I wasn't optimistic.

When my companions and I found the dead animal, the bull still felt warm, so we didn't take time for gutting. We simply split the hide down the backbone and systematically removed meat from the bones. We hung each piece in the shade to cool quickly, and within an hour

Table 1. Weight conversion figures for bull elk.

Weight example	Factor
Whole weight = 582 lb.[a]	1.48 X field dressed weight
FIeld dressed weight = 400 lbs. (viscera removed)	0.675 X whole weight
Clean dressed weight = 332 lb. (skin and head removed)	0.83 X field dressed weight
Packaged retail cuts = 216 lb. (bone left in leg, loin, rib and shoulder cuts)	0.54 X field dressed weight
Packaged cuts (all boneless) = 172 lbs.	0.43 X field dressed weight

[a]Whole weight is used in place of live weight. Whole weight is slightly less than live weight because it does not take into account blood loss at the time of kill. Blood loss on slaughtered steers ranges from 3.04 to 3.70% of the whole weight (Ramsey et al., 1965). According to Reichert and Brown (1909), these amounts are less than half the total blood in the body.

the woods looked like a laundromat. Nothing remained of the elk but a bare skeleton. We didn't lose one ounce of meat off that bull, but if we had followed the normal field-dressing procedure and hung halves or quarters of the animal, I think the meat would have spoiled because it wouldn't have cooled quickly enough to prevent bone sour.

Boning also facilitates handling an elk. Above I've described how to quarter an elk, and that's ideal if a couple of you are working together. But I'm personally not strong enough to handle entire elk quarters by myself. You have to remember that even one quarter of a small bull will weigh 100 pounds or more, and it takes a pretty husky guy to handle that alone.

So when I'm alone, I bone out my elk just to ease the strain. In essence I dismantle an elk, piece by piece. When you first look at a big bull on the ground, you'll shrink back and think, "How can I ever handle that mammoth by myself?" But when you remember you can reduce it to small, easy-to-handle portions, the task seems much less ominous.

That's what I realized in Montana in 1984. I was alone, seven or eight miles from a road, when I shot a very large bull. Even gutting a bull by yourself can be back-breaking labor, and my back wasn't up to that task. So instead I skinned and dismantled the animal right where it lay. The heaviest piece weighed no more than 70 to 80 pounds, and I took that entire bull apart by myself in about two hours, and didn't break my back doing it.

How To Bone

The problem in boning any animal is opening the meat to contamination and drying, so avoid hacking it up helter-skelter. You want to remove large, self-contained chunks, and if you bag these in clean meat sacks, you can keep the boned meat virtually spotless.

Most likely your elk will be lying on its side, so start with it in that position. Don't bother to gut it. Just start skinning at the belly. As you cut the hide here, be careful not to cut into the body cavity. Work to the backbone until you've got half the bull skinned from head to tail. Cut off all the legs at the knees.

Now pull the front leg away from the body and cut it off. Slip it into a clean game bag and lay it aside. (Bag each piece of meat you remove from then on, and hang it or lay it on rocks or logs for quick cooling.)

Next remove the hind leg. To do this, start on the inside of the leg and slide your knife right along the pelvis bone so that all the meat comes off with the leg. Be very careful to keep your knife on the pelvis to avoid

Above, Larry Jones of Springfield, Oregon begins taking apart a cow elk piece-by-piece. To save time and keep the job as clean as possible, he has not gutted the animal. Rather he has just started skinning at the belly. Notice that he has used nylon cord to tie the legs back, out of the way. Below, he has skinned the animal all the way down the backbone from head to tail.

Now Larry pulls back the front leg and cuts it off close to the body.

With the front leg neatly cut off, Larry will slip it into a game bag to keep it clean.

Now Larry removes the hind leg by starting on the inside of the pelvis and sliding his knife close to the pelvic bone. Be careful not to puncture the body cavity on this cut.

The hind leg will come off easily once you've broken the hip joint. It's important to open up this joint for quick cooling because bone sour can spread rapidly from here.

With the legs removed from one side, Larry begins filleting meat off the rib cage starting at the breast bone (brisket).

He continues right to the backbone so the rib meat, neck and backstrap come off in one big slab.

To complete this side, Larry slices meat from between the ribs for use as hamburger. When he's done, even the magpies will have a hard time picking a decent meal off the skeleton!

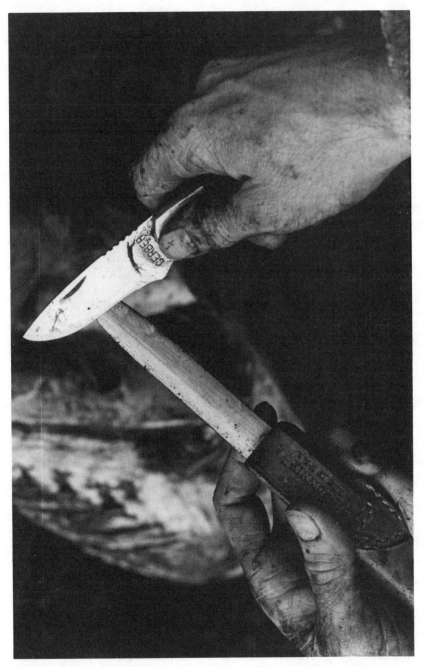

The key to success is a sharp knife! Carry a steel and plan on using it often!

puncturing the body cavity. This is the one place you have to use caution to avoid making a mess. As you cut, continue to push the leg back with your shoulder (or better yet, use your cord to tie the leg back out of your way). Pretty soon you'll come to the ball-and-socket joint in the hip. As you cut the meat loose, the joint will break backwards, and you can finish cutting the leg neatly away from the pelvis.

Now start at the brisket (breast bone) and as if you were filleting a fish, slice the meat off the rib cage, keeping your knife flat against the ribs, and continue right to the back bone. The rib meat, backstrap, flanks and neck meat will come off in one big slab. On a big bull, it may be too heavy to handle easily, so you can cut the neck off to make two lighter pieces. To salvage as much meat as possible, you can cut the strips of meat out from between the ribs. These grind well into hamburger.

Now you can roll the animal over and do exactly the same on the other side. When you've finished skinning and boning, gut the animal to retrieve the tenderloins (on the inside of the backbone between the pelvis and rib cage), heart and liver, and presto, you're done (except for the packing). To further reduce weight, you can bone out the legs. That will reduce the weight of the front legs considerably, but bone makes up a small percentage of the back legs, so I normally leave the hind-leg bones in place. The hams are easier to handle that way.

Camp Time

One important question remains for field care of meat: "How long can you safely hang meat in camp?"

Unfortunately there's no absolute answer because too many variables are involved. Some animals inherently contain more bacteria than others. An animal that was run or frightened just before it died will deteriorate faster than one that was calm. Animals with many meat-contaminating wounds will spoil rapidly. High humidity encourages bacterial growth and rapid spoiling.

However, some rough guidelines may apply. Meat plants generally age beef for two weeks at 35 degrees, and they also quick-age meat for three days at 65 degrees. These parameters don't apply directly to game meat because of the variables mentioned above, but they offer an idea of the outer limits. Commercial meat cutters go by the axiom, "life begins at 40 degrees." If you can cool an animal to 40 degrees within 24 hours and keep it that cold, you can safely hang the meat in camp for as long as two weeks—assuming it's not badly shot up or covered with dirt, or the humidity isn't exceptionally high. With any increase in temperature or contamination, time diminishes. At 65 degrees, you'd better get your elk into cold storage within three days or you may lose it.

There are ways to keep meat cool for long periods, even if daytime temperatures are high. One September I killed a large mule deer buck on the first day of a drop-camp hunt, and our packer wasn't due to make a meat check for seven days. In cold weather that would have been no problem, but in the continual rain and warm temperatures that year, I felt apprehensive. At night the temperature was dropping to about 45 degrees, but during the day it rose to 65.

Each night I hung the skinned and quartered buck to cool, and it always dropped to air temperature (45 degrees). I made a plastic lean-to roof to keep off the rain. First thing each morning I stacked the meat on a tarp and wrapped it with sleeping bags. At the end of each day, after 12 hours in sleeping bags, the internal temperature never rose above 48 degrees, and after seven days in camp, that meat was still as pink and sweet smelling as it had been the first day. Many times I've used that same method in camp with excellent results.

I've also used it to transport meat home. A good insulation of sleeping bags will keep a well-chilled animal cold for three or four days. My friend Roger Iveson and I killed two bulls in Wyoming. Nights in the mountains were getting down to about 30 degrees, so the meat was well chilled. Before setting out we wrapped all the meat together in a tarp and then buried it under sleeping bags. It took three days to reach my home in Oregon, but the meat was still down around 40 degrees when we arrived.

Here's one important point about transporting meat in a pickup bed: The exhaust system will make the floor of the bed warm enough to spoil meat, so always put down a thick foam mattress or other insulation under the meat.

In some cases the weather in camp may not get cold enough to cool an animal well, even at night. If you can't get meat out immediately, store it in a creek bottom or a shaded draw. Cold air moves downhill so the bottom of a draw will be the coldest place around. And many mountain creeks run at 45 degrees or colder, so the cool air over a creek will help to cool meat down.

Finally, always prepare for the worst of circumstances, and if you're going into backcountry during warm weather, arrange for an outfitter to pack out your meat, and never shoot an animal in a situation where you're not positive you can retrieve it. Big antlers and horns get all the notice, but the real proof of hunting savvy appears on the table. Killing a trophy animal becomes a hollow accomplishment if you lose the meat.

To Age Or Not To Age?

Another often-debated meat care subject is aging. All meat contains enzymes that function even after an animal has died. Connective tissue between cells and muscles is largely responsible for toughness, and the action of enzymes softens these tissues. Albert Levie in the *Meat Handbook* describes the process this way: "A medical suture is a dramatic example of enzymatic action. Strands of sheep gut are frequently used, which consist chiefly of collagen (connective tissue). These stitches that disappear are hydrolyzed by the enzymes in the body." Similar action takes place during aging, and in the process it tenderizes meat.

Studies in Wyoming show that the ideal age periods, provided the meat is cooled to 40 degrees, are seven days for cow elk and 14 for bulls.

Generally, the higher the temperature the faster the aging process. Levie again states: "By increasing the temperature, it is roughly estimated that what requires 12 days to achieve at 32 degrees can be achieved at 42 degrees in six days, 48 degrees in four days, and 60 degrees in two days."

It should be re-emphasized that at warmer temperatures, bacteria and molds grow rapidly on the surface of a carcass. Not only does meat age faster under warmer conditions, but it spoils faster, too. Thus, an animal hung in camp at 60 degrees for two days, for example, not only requires no further aging, but it must be cut and frozen immediately to prevent spoilage.

Ray Field points out that young animals—yearlings—are inherently tender and need no aging. In addition, the meat of animals that have been stressed or badly shot up is subject to rapid bacterial growth and will spoil quickly, so it should not be aged.

To ensure tender meat, it's also important to wait until an animal is thoroughly cooled before cutting it up. If meat is still warm with body heat, and you cut it cross-grain, the muscles will constrict and you'll end up with steaks so tough your dog can't chew them. One time I cut the tenderloin out of a buck deer, and being very hungry, I sliced a couple of steaks off the tenderloin to cook immediately over a fire. The meat coiled up like a spring, and I had to bite with all my strength to tear off little strips. The rest of the deer, cut up after it had cooled, was very tender. Wait at least 12 hours before butchering your elk, even if it's a young, tender one that requires no aging.

How To Freeze Elk Meat

Freezing is the important last step in meat care. You can take your animal to a butcher shop, where it will be sawed into cuts similar to those of beef, but I think you can do a better job yourself.

Double wrap your meat and freeze it at 0° F. You'll enjoy fine eating for many months to come.

Regardless of how you've handled it in the field, I suggest you bone it for freezing. That way you remove all bone, which saves freezer space, and you also can trim the meat spotlessly clean, which guarantees good flavor. Once you've reduced it to the large pieces described in the earlier section on boning, dissect it along natural muscle lines. The hams and front legs come apart in neat muscle groups. Trim off all fat, which can turn rancid even in a freezer, and cut off all blood shot and tainted places that can produce off flavor.

Cut the meat into meal-sized packages. I generally cut the choice portions into roasts and freeze them in whole pieces, rather than cutting them into steaks. The less surface area exposed, the less drying that will take place. When these roasts are thawed they can be cooked whole, or while still partially frozen, they can be sliced into steaks. Save the neck, flanks and scrap meat for stew meat, jerky and hamburger.

Now wrap each piece of meat first in plastic wrap, and then with coated freezer paper. The plastic ensures an air-tight seal, which prevents dehydration. Game meat wrapped this way will stay fresh for at least a year. A couple of times I've inadvertently overlooked elk roasts in my freezer for two years. I've hesitated to eat these, but not wanting to waste meat I've tried them, and the meat has tasted as if it came off a freshly killed animal.

It's important to freeze meat at zero degrees or lower. At 20 degrees, bacteria can still grow, but at zero bacterial growth ceases. Also, ground meat with mixed-in fat, and cured meats with fat and salt, will turn rancid under freezing conditions, so these should be frozen for no more than six months or so.

11

Hunting For
A Trophy Bull

What Is A Trophy?

For many hunters, killing an elk, any elk, will always be thrill enough, and the need to kill a "trophy" never arises. Other hunters, if they've hunted elk a lot, tire of taking smaller elk and start holding out for mature bulls, or maybe even a 6-point or nothing. Still others go beyond that point and evaluate elk in terms of record book measurements, and they set their sights above the average mature bull and begin their search for a record-book animal.

The question then must be answered: What is a trophy bull? "A trophy is in the eye of the beholder" has been said so many times it has become a trite phrase, yet it still contains some truth. When I first started elk hunting, I killed a couple of cow elk, and no animals have ever given me a bigger thrill. Indeed, at the time those were truly trophy animals to me.

Even given that truth, some objective standard must be set to define "trophy." Probably to most hunters, any 6-point bull would qualify as a trophy animal, and certainly any hunter should be happy with any mature bull. That still doesn't define "trophy" adequately, though, because even among mature 6-point bulls, the variation can be great.

The minimum qualifying scores for the record books are not an adequate measure. The minimum score for the Pope and Young record book is 265 (score is a total of width, length, tine lengths, and beam circumferences, which will be explained fully further on). A bull that measures 265 is a decent bull in anybody's book, and it's a fine trophy

The definition of "trophy" can vary greatly. To some hunters this would be a trophy bull, and to others it's little more than a raghorn.

for a bowhunter, but compared to a bull that makes the Boone and Crockett record book, for which the minimum is 375, a 265-point bull appears rather modest.

In general terms, most serious hunters who have seen a lot of elk would consider a bull that scores 300 or higher, based on the Boone and Crockett measuring system, a good trophy, and I would agree with that. A bull of that magnitude has long main beams, a good spread, long tines, fairly heavy antlers, and well represents its species. However, most areas, regardless of hunting pressure, feed, escape cover or other parameters are capable of growing bulls of that size, so 300 is not even a good breakoff point for a discussion of locating a trophy area.

For the sake of this discussion, I'll define a trophy bull as a Boone and Crockett bull, that is, a bull that measures 375 or more. That standard takes in the cream of the crop, the best of the best, and it eliminates the possibility of subjective judgement, that is, the "eye of the beholder" syndrome. The quality of a 375 bull is not relative to anyone's hunting experience or goals. That's a big animal no matter who took it and where they killed it, and bulls like that don't grow just anywhere. They're restricted to unique locations that provide just the right mix of genes, food, shelter and other elements. An animal of that magnitude is simply in the top percentile, and that defines it as a trophy bull.

This isn't to say that the following discussion has value only if you're after a Boone and Crockett bull. The same principles that apply to planning for such an animal apply to finding a lesser trophy as well. And besides, if you locate those places that can potentially produce Boone and Crockett bulls, your chances for taking a larger than average bull, even if it falls short of the record book, are better than average.

Many guides and outfitters offer "trophy" hunts. Make sure you understand what this means before you book such a hunt in hopes of taking a record-book animal. Many heavily guided regions grow few record-class elk, and some of the best trophy-bull areas have no guides, so "trophy hunt" and "record-book hunt" aren't necessarily synonymous.

In addition, guides must maintain a fairly high success rate to maintain a favorable reputation, so few will take clients to hunt specifically for record-book animals. If they did, their clients would rarely kill an elk and they would look like real bozo guides.

The guided "trophy hunt" generally means you'll have an opportunity to shoot a mature bull elk or to take one of the best bulls the guide's area produces. That's more than enough to satisfy most hunters, but just understand that it probably doesn't mean you'll have a chance to shoot, or even see, a record-book elk. Therefore, I think hunting *expressly* for a *record-book* elk can be considered a do-it-yourself project.

Many outfitters offer "trophy elk hunts", but be sure you know what that means. Does it mean you're hunting for a Boone & Crockett bull, or only that you'll have chances to kill a mature elk?

The Parameters Of A Trophy Area

Several "trophy factors" come into play, and some are more important than others. It could be misleading to rank them in terms of importance, because none really stands alone. It's a matter of laying out all the pieces and studying each one until the shapes and colors begin to mesh. For the sake of simplicity, however, some form of organization has to be applied, so I'll rank trophy factors in the order I think is most significant.

The most valuable point of departure for trophy research is the Boone and Crockett book, *Records Of North American Big Game* because it reflects the areas that produce the largest elk. By analyzing the listings in this book, you can draw some conclusions on where the biggest bulls are found, or at least where they've been taken in the past.

Heredity. Any state has the potential to produce the odd trophy bull, but without question some states have greater potential than others, and specific regions within those states probably produce most of the biggest elk. Locating these specific areas is the first step in successful trophy elk hunting.

Age apparently is not the major ingredient in a trophy bull. In some areas, elk reach trophy proportions in a relatively short period of time, whereas in other areas, the oldest bulls never reach record book class. Heredity may be the single most important element, because a herd must have the right blood lines to produce oversized bulls. However, other factors such as mineral content of the soil and range quality are involved, too.

For example, the Eagle Cap Wilderness covers nearly a half-million acres at the heart of Oregon's Wallowa Mountains. Although this back-country region gets fairly heavy pressure from outfitters and their clients, the country is remote enough to prevent overharvest, and the area contains a number of mature bulls. The bull-cow ratio runs somewhere between 15 and 20 bulls per 100 cows, which means that good numbers of mature bulls survive from year to year. I've hunted this region many times and have observed dozens of mature bulls, yet I've never seen one that would score much over 300, if that much. I asked big game biologist Vic Coggins why few of the bulls there attain huge size.

"Lack of winter range is the main problem," Coggins said. "The elk have plenty of summer range, but when winter snow drives them from that high country, they have only a narrow fringe of timber around the base of the mountains to hold them through the winter. Food production there is poor, and they get a poor start on antler growth in the spring."

As a result, even bulls that live long enough to die of old age rarely grow truly trophy racks.

At the Vermejo Ranch in New Mexico, elk have been managed for decades strictly for trophy quality. Writing in the *Bugle,* the journal of the Rocky Mountain Elk Foundation, Gary Wolfe, game manager at Vermejo, points out that over a period of time 482 bull elk killed by hunters have been evaluated in terms of age and antler measurements. Of the 482 bulls killed, 48 scored 300 or better. Thirty-six of those bulls were between 7½ and 10½ years old, the age range that produces the biggest bulls, but the largest bull measured only 353 ⅝. Maybe it's not

New Mexico produces some very fine elk as is proven by this bull. But overall, very few Boone & Crockett bulls have been recorded in New Mexico.

fair to say the largest scored "only 353" because that's a fine animal, but still it falls far short of Boone and Crockett's minimum. And this is on a huge block of land managed to grow the largest possible bulls. It would appear that some natural limitations, whether lack of winter range, poor minerals or the wrong heredity, limits the maximum size of bulls.

The same can be said for New Mexico in general. This state contains a number of old Spanish Land Grant ranches similar to Vermejo, along with a couple of Indian reservations that manage for trophy hunting. If any state has the land-use patterns to produce old, trophy bulls,

New Mexico does, yet only four bulls from that state are listed in the 8th Edition of *Records Of North American Big Game*, which indicates a lack of one or more elements, other than old age, required to produce huge bulls.

Here's a breakdown of the total numbers of elk listed from each state or province in the 8th Edition of *Records Of North American Big Game:*

Record Book Bulls by State	
Montana	61
Wyoming	43
Alberta	29
Colorado	27
Idaho	24
Arizona	18
Oregon	6
New Mexico	4

A scattering of bulls from Saskatchewan, Manitoba, Texas and unknown also are listed.

Those raw figures hint at trophy potential, and generally speaking, the states with the highest number of record book entries may offer the best chance for a trophy bull. However, that must be qualified to be of much value, and a couple of variables, other than absolute numbers, must be considered.

Odds. These can be figured roughly by comparing the number of record book entries against the total number of elk killed in each state. Jack and Susan Reneau, in their intriguing book, *Colorado's Biggest Bucks and Bulls*, analyze trophy potential in terms of the odds. They make a ratio of the Boone and Crockett entries and the total number of elk killed to estimate the odds for taking a Boone and Crockett bull in each state. Their findings point out the distinct gap between quantity and quality.

For example, Arizona, with 18 entries, ranks only sixth in terms of total entries in Boone and Crockett, which doesn't look so great until you consider that annual harvest rarely exceeds 2,000 animals, or roughly one-tenth the harvest in most major elk states. Weighing Boone and Crockett entries against total harvest, the Reneaus figure the odds for taking a record-book bull in Arizona are 1 in 1,916, the best for any state. Odds for the more famous elk states shape up this way: 1 in 11,969 in Wyoming; 1 in 13,736 in Idaho; and 1 in 14,910 in Colorado. The

Reneaus didn't compute odds for Montana and Alberta, two of the top three elk producers, probably because no long-term harvest data were available. I suspect, however, considering annual harvest and the total number of Boone and Crockett entries, that the odds for Alberta, where annual harvest rarely exceeds 1,500 animals, would be similar to or better than those for Arizona, and for Montana they would be a little lower—because the annual elk kill is much higher—but still somewhat better than Wyoming.

Age. The other major "if" in record book study is the date. If all bulls listed in the book were killed before 1960, you know something has probably changed to erode the trophy potential. It could be that range or other habitat conditions have changed, but more likely the land, hunting regulations, or hunting pressure have changed so that fewer bulls are living long enough to reach trophy proportions these days. Bulls must live at least 6½ years to reach maximum size, and studies have shown—for example those at Vermejo Park—that most bulls reach maximum size at ages from 7½ to 10½ years old.

Wherever large herds of elk attract lots of hunters and accessibility is good, the turnover of bulls is rapid. For example, in some units of Northeastern Oregon, 80 percent or more of the bulls killed each year are yearlings, and very few bulls live longer than three or four years. The same holds true for parts of the popular White River National Forest in Colorado. These areas may have the needed blood lines and feed to grow Boone and Crockett bulls, but few if any animals survive long enough to grow 5-point racks, let alone trophy antlers. Any branch-antlered bull from these regions would be considered big.

Bull-Cow Ratio. Perhaps the most reliable indicator of the age of bulls is the bull-cow ratio. Rather than counting actual numbers, biologists compute the number of bulls in relation to a given number of cows. In general the lower the percentage of bulls, the younger the average age of the bulls. In those units of Oregon and Colorado, for example, where 80 percent of the bulls killed are yearlings, the bull-cow ratio following hunting seasons each fall ranges between five and 10 bulls per 100 cows. The chances of seeing any kind of mature bull in an area where the bull-cow ratio is five bulls per 100 cows is remote.

Roughly speaking, the higher the bull-cow ratio, the older the average age of the bulls. If you're looking strictly for a trophy bull, you probably wouldn't want to hunt an area with a bull-cow ratio lower than 15 to 20 bulls per 100 cows, and many experienced hunters feel a ratio of 30 bulls per 100 cows or higher is required for an area to qualify as a major trophy locality.

Bull-cow ratios are affected most directly by hunting, and for an area to maintain a high ratio, the number of hunters must be limited in some way. That's the case on some private ranches and Indian reservations. The Fort Apache Indian Reservation in Arizona has wisely adopted a selective-hunting policy designed to produce trophy bulls, and right now it may rank as the best place in North America to kill a Boone and Crockett bull—provided you've got enough money to pay the price.

If you can't afford to hunt that kind of operation, you can look for other situations that might afford the protection needed to grow old bulls. The most obvious would be wilderness country. The inaccessible nature of much wilderness necessarily limits the number of hunters. That doesn't mean, however, that huge wilderness areas are necessarily ideal spots for Boone and Crockett bulls. Some wilderness country simply doesn't have the right heredity and the needed feed to grow outsized bulls, and just as important, much deep wilderness is more heavily hunted than you might think. Virtually all major wilderness areas support large numbers of outfitters, and most wilderness rifle seasons run from mid-September through November. There may not be a lot of hunters at any one time, but the total hunting effort is fairly great, especially when you consider that outfitters know their country intimately and can produce a much higher-than-average success for their clients.

For that reason, I'm inclined to shy away from true wilderness and look more to fringe country. This may be the border areas at the edges of wilderness areas, or they could be roadless drainages or ridges sandwiched between road-accessible reaches. Most of these areas are too small for outfitters to work, but they're too rugged for the average foot hunter, so they're an in-between never land where bulls can live out their lives with a minimum of harassment.

Any extremely rough or brushy country holds the promise of a big bull. In planning a hunt, study maps to locate the kinds of places where other hunters either wouldn't consider hunting because of the terrible conditions, or look for places they might simply overlook because the locations seem too obvious. When you've got a few places lined up, talk to local biologists to assess the bull-cow ratios. Often the percentage of bulls may be low on the average for an entire game management unit, but specific drainages within that unit might maintain a high ratio.

It doesn't matter whether hunting pressure is restricted by natural barriers as discussed above, or whether it's man-imposed, and hunting regulations in themselves can lead to quality trophy hunting. Arizona presents a prime example. The number of elk tags there for all hunts—rifle, bow, and muzzleloader—have been limited in number for many years. As a result, the entire state in essence is a controlled-permit area, and hunting pressure is held low enough so that a high percentage of bulls live to old age.

The same principle operates on a smaller scale in other states. Colorado has set aside more than 20 management units across the state as quality areas. The number of permits authorized for each unit is severely restricted to improve bull-cow ratios, and these units promise to bloom as super spots for trophy bulls. Other states have similar quota hunts where the potential for a big bull is far above average. The obvious drawback is that you're never sure whether you'll get a permit, but if you're willing to put up with that hassle, your chances for a better-than-average bull are excellent.

The Opportune Time. Other variables in trophy hunting are the time of year and hunting method. Under some conditions elk are extremely hard to locate and hunt, and under other conditions they're relatively easy. The hunting method and time of year you choose could greatly influence your potential for taking a trophy bull.

As I pointed out in the chapter on bugling, hunting during the rut not only can be exciting, but it gives you an edge over the largest bulls. That's when they're most active and most easily located because of their bugling, and that's also a time they've lost some of their native caution. As a result, hunting during the rut improves your odds greatly. That's true whether you're hunting with bow or rifle.

Late seasons when deep snow drives elk from remote high country and concentrates them in more accessible areas, and when snow makes them more visible and easy to track, also present good conditions for trophy hunting. Many outfitters charge more for early bugle hunts and late snow hunts around Thanksgiving than they do for October time slots, because they know the early and late periods offer the best trophy potential.

In hunting specifically for a trophy, it's important to choose methods that allow time to look over a bull. Again, bugling is conducive to trophy hunting because you often can pull a bull in fairly close and get a good look at him.

During late seasons, when many trees have shed their leaves and snow covers the ground, you often can look over animals well enough to judge antler dimensions.

Duwane Adams, a trophy hunter from Arizona, uses the same spotting techniques for elk in Colorado he uses for Coues and mule deer in the deserts of southern Arizona, and he has had opportunity to look over hundreds of elk where most hunters would see few if any. He sets his 15X60 Zeiss binoculars on a tripod, and from one side of a canyon he sits for hours studying the far side of the canyon. He not only spots

Bugling gives the trophy hunter an added edge. Hunting in late season's snow also puts the odds a bit more in his favor.

many elk this way, but he has time to evaluate the trophy quality of each bull.

Judging Trophy Quality In The Field

To hunt trophy elk seriously, you must be able to gauge the dimensions of a rack at a glance. Some experienced measurers can glance at a rack and guess the score within five inches or less. *That takes practice.* The rough dimensions given below will help you develop your own system for field judging, but it takes practice to perfect your eye, so measure elk racks whenever the opportunity arises. Experience is the only reliable teacher.

Perhaps the first consideration for record-book elk is the number of tines. Some 5-point bulls will score well enough to make the Pope and Young Club's minimum score of 265, and an exceptional 5-point will measure better than 300, but that's rare. For practical purposes, you can assume that a bull must have at least 6-points on a side to make any record book, and many of the elk listed in Boone and Crockett have seven or more points to the side. Fifteen of the top 20 bulls listed in the 8th Edition of *Records Of North American Big Game* are measured at least as 7X7s. The score chart allows measurement of as many as eight points per side (actually seven tines plus the main beam).

To determine the number of points quickly in the field, you don't need to count them individually. Unless the rack is formed abnormally, the sword point—the long one that points straight up—is always the fourth tine. You simply spot that tine and count from there. If the bull has two more points, it's a 6-point; if it has three more, it's a 7-point.

Remember that a bull must have at least six points on both sides to be measured as a 6-point. As we'll see below in the section on measuring a rack, the difference in score between one side and the other is subtracted from the total score. In essence then, a 5 x 6 rack is measured as a 5 x 5.

I learned the value of symmetry first-hand on a bull I killed in Montana. As the elk approached, I could see it would place well up in the Pope and Young record book, so I didn't hesitate to shoot it.

But when I walked up to the bull, I noticed that one brow tine had been broken off cleanly. With both brow tines, the bull would have been an even 6 x 6 and would have measured 310 to 315. With one missing brow tine, the bull in essence became a 5 x 5 and scored only 280. That's because the rack not only lost about 16 inches for the broken-off tine (I'm assuming the tine would have been 16 inches long to match the other brow tine), but the length of the tine on the other side also had to

A pair of tripod-mounted binoculars or a spotting scope are invaluable when it comes to spotting bulls and evaluating their racks.

be subtracted, so the total loss of score for one missing 16-inch tine was 32 inches.

The same is true for any lack of symmetry. If a tine grows from an abnormal location, it must be subtracted from the total score. That's why symmetry is important if you're strictly after a high-scoring bull. To gauge the total score of an asymmetrical bull in the field, say a 5 x 7, simply judge the score of the weaker side and double it, and you come out fairly close.

Primary measurements are length of main beams, inside spread, length of tines, and mass. The most important measurements in terms of overall score are length of main beams and cumulative lengths of points. Spread and mass (circumference measurements) contribute, of course, but they make up a relatively small percentage of the total score, so you first want to judge the main beam length and tine quality.

Mike Cupell, who measures for Boone and Crockett, Pope and Young, and several state and local record books in Arizona, uses body measurements to help gauge the size of an elk's rack. The chest of a mature bull measures 22 to 24 inches wide and 36 to 40 inches deep. Distance from the base of the antlers to the tip of the nose is 15 to 16 inches. A mature bull elk stands about 60 inches high at the shoulder, and body length from the base of the neck to the tail is about 60 inches. These measurements can be used as a rough ruler in gauging dimensions of a rack.

So many variables enter into the score of a rack, it's impossible to lay down absolutes. However, most bulls in the Boone and Crockett book (minimum score 375) have a main beam length of at least 50 inches and in many cases the beams exceed 55 inches. Spread varies greatly, but a majority of Boone and Crockett bulls have an inside spread of at least 40 inches, and many are 45 to 50 inches wide. In rough terms, then, if you see a bull with 50-inch beams—nearly as long as the body—and an inside spread greater than 40 inches—more than twice the width of the chest—you know the bull at least has the overall dimensions to make the book.

You often hear hunters say, "That bull was so big his antlers hung over his rump as he ran." That makes a good story, but it's not true. As I've said, a bull measures about 60 inches from the base of his neck to his tail. Of course, his head rides some distance forward of the base of the neck, and in addition, the main beams aren't straight; much of the main-beam length comes from curvature, so even on a bull with 60-inch main beams, the straight-line length is probably closer to 50 inches. In order for a bull's antlers to reach his rump, he would have

Use body dimensions to help make quick judgements of elk racks. For example, a bull's chest measures nearly 24 inches thick. This bull's rack is at least twice as wide as his chest, so his inside spread is probably close to 48 inches!

to have an awfully short neck or 80-inch main beams. That may not be impossible, but it's close.

Tine length plays a big part in score. Mike Cupell says if you see a bull with brow tines that run straight out as far as the end of the nose and then curve up, you're looking at a good one. If the nose is 16 inches long, then those brow tines would be longer than 20 inches. The second and third tines should be equally long, and the fourth—sword—point should be 24 inches or longer. The fifth tine should equal the third, and the sixth point—actually the end of the main beam—should be longer than the fifth point. If you see a bull with those dimensions, you know you're looking at a record-class bull.

Many bulls have exceptional first, second and fourth points, but the third and fifth points are weak. Short tines can take many inches off a score, so look at those points carefully.

To qualify for the Pope and Young archery record book a bull must score well in all the same areas, but with smaller dimensions. Roughly speaking, a Pope and Young bull, given at least six points on each side, must have 40-inch main beams and a 35-inch inside spread, and the first three points must be 15 inches long or longer. Of course, there are hundreds of variations on that theme, but a bull of those general dimensions will get you in the bowhunter's record book.

Measuring And Submitting A Trophy Rack

If you've never measured antlers, you probably think the scoring system is some kind of hokus pokus devised by a mad scientist, but with a little experience you'll discover it's straightforward and simple. The only equipment you need is a quarter-inch-wide steel tape measure. One tape with a hook on the end is adequate, but another tape with a ring on the end helps in measuring circumferences. In addition you need a copy of the score chart (use the one in this book), and it also helps if someone else holds the antlers and writes down scores as you measure.

Steps for measuring a rack are outlined on the score charts, but differences in technique can make significant differences in score, so a standard procedure is essential.

Before you start, note a couple of points about the scoring system. You can measure your trophy in the field to get a rough idea of score, but to have it measured officially for record-book consideration, you must let the rack dry under normal conditions for at least 60 days.

Also notice that all fractions are measured and recorded to the nearest ⅛ inch. To keep addition simple, they are not reduced to the lowest common denominator.

Non-Counting Measurements. Measurements A, B, and C on the score chart do not count toward the official score, but they're required for a complete record. On line A you record the number of points on each side. A point is any projection more than an inch long, but the length of the projection must exceed the diameter of the base. In other words, if it's wider at the base than it is long, it's not counted as a point. The method for determining the base of a point will be discussed below under "Tine Measurement."

On Line B you record the distance between the antler tips, and on Line C you record the greatest outside spread. In some cases this could be measured from the outside of one main beam to the outside of the other, but often on elk, points will flare out beyond the main beams, and then the measurement is taken between the most widely flared points.

Inside Spread. Measurement D, inside spread of the main beams, is the width measurement that really counts. Place the end of your tape on the inside of one main beam and extend it across to the other. Slide the tape up and down until you've determined the widest point between the beams. Caution: This measurement must be taken at a 90-degree angle to a line drawn straight up from the skull. In other words, be careful not to take a diagonal measurement.

OFFICIAL SCORING SYSTEM FOR NORTH AMERICAN BIG GAME TROPHIES

Records of North American Big Game	BOONE AND CROCKETT CLUB	P.O. Box 547 Dumfries, VA 22026

Minimum Score: Awards 360 All-time 375

TYPICAL AMERICAN ELK (WAPITI)

DETAIL OF POINT MEASUREMENT

	Abnormal Points	
	Right Antler	Left Antler
E. Total of Lengths of Abnormal Points		

SEE OTHER SIDE FOR INSTRUCTIONS		Column 1	Column 2	Column 3	Column 4
A. No. Points on Right Antler	No. Points on Left Antler	Spread Credit	Right Antler	Left Antler	Difference
B. Tip to Tip Spread	C. Greatest Spread				
D. Inside Spread of Main Beams	(Credit May Equal But Not Exceed Longer Antler)				
F. Length of Main Beam					
G-1. Length of First Point					
G-2. Length of Second Point					
G-3. Length of Third Point					
G-4. Length of Fourth (Royal) Point					
G-5. Length of Fifth Point					
G-6. Length of Sixth Point, If Present					
G-7. Length of Seventh Point, If Present					
H-1. Circumference at Smallest Place Between First and Second Points					
H-2. Circumference at Smallest Place Between Second and Third Points					
H-3. Circumference at Smallest Place Between Third and Fourth Points					
H-4. Circumference at Smallest Place Between Fourth and Fifth Points					
TOTALS					

Enter Total of Columns 1, 2, and 3		Exact Locality Where Killed:	
Subtract Column 4		Date Killed:	By Whom Killed:
Subtotal		Present Owner:	
Subtract (E) Total of Lengths of Abn. Points		Guide Name and Address:	
FINAL SCORE		Remarks:	

This is an official Boone & Crockett score chart which details their copyrighted measuring system. (Reprinted with permission of the Boone & Crockett Club.)

I certify that I have measured the above trophy on _____ 19 _____

at (address) _____ City _____ State _____
and that these measurements and data are, to the best of my knowledge and belief, made In accordance with the
Instructions given.

Witness: _____ Signature _____

B&C OFFICIAL MEASURER

I.D. Number

INSTRUCTIONS FOR MEASURING TYPICAL AMERICAN ELK (WAPITI)

All measurements must be made with a 1/4-inch flexible steel tape to the nearest one-eighth of an inch. Wherever
It Is necessary to change direction of measurement, mark a control point and swing tape at this point. (Note: a
flexible steel cable can be used to measure points and main beams only.) Enter fractional figures in eighths,
without reduction. Official measurements cannot be taken until the antlers have dried for at least 60 days after
the animal was killed.

A. Number of Points on Each Antler: to be counted a point, the projection must be at least one inch long, with
length exceeding width at one inch or more of length. All points are measured from tip of point to nearest edge
of beam as Illustrated. Beam tip is counted as a point but not measured as a point.

B. Tip to Tip Spread Is measured between tips of main beams.

C. Greatest Spread is measured between perpendiculars at a right angle to the center line of the skull at widest
part, whether across main beams or points.

D. Inside Spread of Main Beams Is measured at a right angle to the center line of the skull at widest point
between main beams. Enter this measurement again as Spread Credit If It is less than or equal to the length of
longer antler; If longer, enter longer antler length for Spread Credit.

E. Total of Lengths of all Abnormal Points: Abnormal Points are those non-typical In location (such as points
originating from a point or from bottom or sides of main beam) or pattern (extra points, not generally paired).
Measure In usual manner and record In appropriate blanks.

F. Length of Main Beam Is measured from lowest outside edge of burr over outer curve to the most distant point of
what Is, or appears to be, the main beam. The point of beginning is that point on the burr where the center line
along the outer curve of the beam Intersects the burr, then following generally the line of the Illustration.

G. 1-2-3-4-5-6-7 Length of Normal Points: Normal points project from the top or front of the main beam In the
general pattern Illustrated. They are measured from nearest edge of main beam over outer curve to tip. Lay the
tape along the outer curve of the beam so that the top edge of the tape coincides with the top edge of the beam
on both sides of point to determine the baseline for point measurement. Record point length In appropriate
blanks.

H. 1-2-3-4 Circumferences are taken as detailed for each measurement.

* * * * * * * * * * * * * * * * *

FAIR CHASE STATEMENT FOR ALL HUNTER-TAKEN TROPHIES

To make use of the following methods shall be deemed as UNFAIR CHASE and unsportsmanlike, and any trophy
obtained by use of such means is disqualified from entry.

  I. Spotting or herding game from the air, followed by landing In Its vicinity for pursuit;

 II. Herding or pursuing game with motor-powered vehicles;

III. Use of electronic communications for attracting, locating or observing game, or guiding the
      hunter to such game;

 IV. Hunting game confined by artificial barriers, including escape-proof fencing; or hunting game
      transplanted solely for the purpose of commercial shooting.

* * * * * * * * * * * * * * * * *

I certify that the trophy scored on this chart was not taken In UNFAIR CHASE as defined above by the Boone
and Crockett Club. I further certify that it was taken In full compliance with local game laws of the
state, province, or territory.

Date _____ Signature of Hunter _____

(Have signature notarized by a Notary Public)

**To be an official Boone & Crockett trophy, a bull must have been taken under fair chase
methods and scored by an offical B&C scorer. (Reprinted with permission of the Boone &
Crockett Club.)**

Note especially the relationship of this measurement to main-beam length. If spread exceeds length of the longer main beam, you enter the beam length on this line rather than spread. In other words, you're penalized for excessive spread. That's unusual on elk, but it can happen.

Abnormal Points. Line E calls for the cumulative length of all abnormal points. This figure is subtracted from the total score, and here again this points out of importance of symmetry. As described above, a point is any projection more than an inch long and that is longer than the width of its base.

This line may generate more discussion among official measurers than any other, because determining "abnormal" often becomes a matter of subjective judgment. In general, elk have a normal configuration of first, second and third tines and then the sword point as the fourth tine. Beyond that they normally have fifth, sixth and seventh points. As the official score chart shows, these tines grow off the top of the main beam. Any tine that grows from a position other than those shown on the chart must be counted as abnormal unless identical tines grow from each main beam. In some cases, matching "abnormal" points are considered normal and are added to the score, rather than subtracted.

Main Beam Measurement. On Line F, it's important to determine the proper starting point. Measurements must be taken along the outer curve, so hold the antlers so you get a direct side view. A line drawn directly through the eye socket to the burr (base) of the antler marks the correct starting point.

Hook the end of your tape on the burr at that point and extend the tape up the beam, always keeping it on the outside crest of the antler. Follow the natural ridges on the antler as a guide. As long as the beam is straight, continue to extend your tape in a straight line. However, when the beam curves even slightly, you must mark that point with a pencil and turn your tape. For example, the first 12 inches may be straight and then the antler may begin to curve. Extend the tape straight out for 12 inches, and then make a pencil mark at the 12-inch point. Keeping the 12-inch point on the tape exactly on the pencil mark, turn the tape and extend it up the beam. If the antler continues to curve, make another mark at 13 inches, turn the tape and extend it, make another mark at 14 inches, turn the tape and extend it and so forth out to the end.

Tine Measurements. Points are listed on the score chart as G-1, G-2, G-3, and so forth out to G-7. Notice that the last point is measured as part of the main beam. To determine the base of the tine, lay your steel tape along the main beam and curve it around the tine you want to measure. Make a pencil mark along the edge of the tape, which marks the base of the tine.

Brow tines are a good gauge of score. You can judge their length against nose length. If they extend straight to the tip of the nose, then curve up, they're probably over 20 inches. These brow tines are 18 inches. The rack has 50-inch main beams and a 44-inch inside spread, but the third and fifth tines are very short which knocks the score down considerably. In the field you must learn to spot such weaknesses.

Measure from that line up the outside curve of the tine. As in measuring the main beam, always keep your tape on the crest of the tine to get the maximum possible distance. If the tine curves to one side or the other, mark it with a pencil and turn the tape just as you did in measuring the main beams. Follow this procedure on each typical point and record these on the appropriate lines.

Circumferences. The circumference measurements are listed as H-1 through H-4 on the score chart. The score chart shows where to take these four measurements. The only trick is to keep your tape at a 90-degree angle to the antler. In other words, be careful not to measure diagonally.

You can use a hook-end tape, but the ring-end tape is better suited for these measurements because it isn't numbered right down to the end. Loop your tape around the antler and work it up and down until you come to the narrowest point. Always try to find the smallest point and record that measurement on the appropriate line.

With these measurements completed, you total up Columns 2 and 3 to get a raw score. Notice, however, that you must record that difference between Column 2 and 3 in Column 4. For example, if one brow tine measures 19 inches, and the other measured 22, the difference is three inches, and you must record this difference in Column 4. When

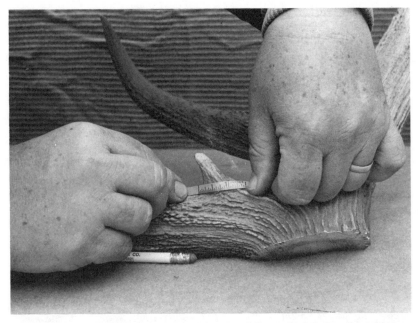

Above, this point is considered normal because it is one inch in length and longer than its base is wide. Below, this point is considered abnormal, because it grows off the side of the main beam instead of the top, which is the normal position.

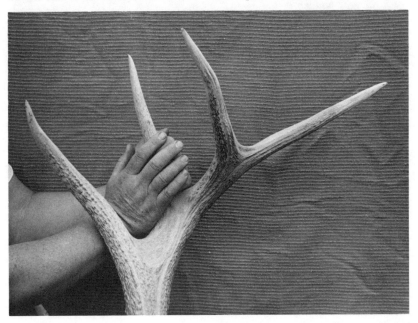

Above, measure the main beam, start at the burr and measure along the outside curve. A line drawn through the eye socket to the base of the antler shows you where to start the measurement. Below, anywhere the beam curves, mark the antler with a pencil. Turn your tape, measure another inch and mark the antler again, turn the tape and so forth.

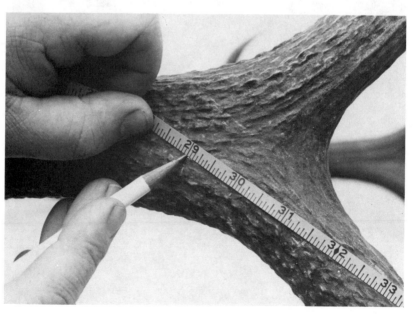

Above, the main beam is actually the sixth point on a six-point bull. Keep your tape along the outside curve right to the tip of the antler to get the maximum allowable measurement. Below, to determine the base of a tine correctly, curve the tape around the tine so that it serves as a projection of the main beam. Make a pencil mark along the tape. That mark is the point from which to measure the tine.

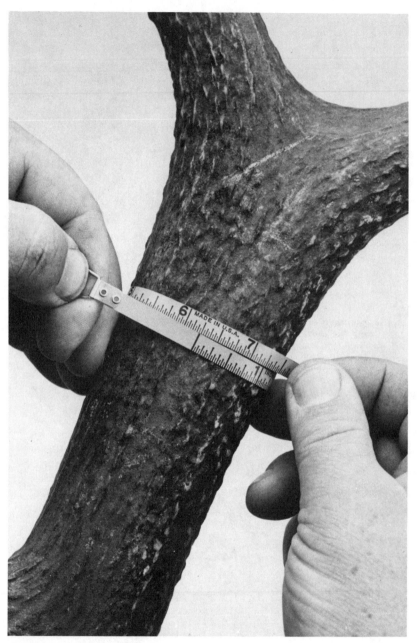

To measure circumference, wrap your tape around the antler and work it up and down until you've found the narrowest point. Make sure your tape is perpendicular to the antler.

you've filled out each blank in Column 4, add them all together. This total must be subtracted from the raw score to give you an actual net score.

Entering A Trophy In The Book. After you've measured your trophy, you'll have a pretty good idea of whether it will make one of the record books. If you think it will, call the nearest official measurer to have the rack scored formally. If you don't know anyone who measures for the record books contact the Boone and Crockett Club (or Pope and Young if you're a bowhunter) to get the names of measurers in your vicinity (addresses for these clubs are listed below).

If your animal qualifies for either record book, you must sign a fair-chase affidavit, which verifies that you took the animal by legal means under the rules of fair chase. Along with the affidavit and the official score chart, you must submit a processing fee and three photos of the rack—right, front and left views.

The Record Keepers

Boone And Crockett. When Theodore Roosevelt traveled to the West in the early 1880s, he witnessed vast desecration of valuable natural resources. He was so appalled that when he returned to the East, he called together some of the nation's most prestigious leaders, and in 1887 they established the Boone and Crockett Club, not as a records-keeping organization, but as a conservation group to lobby for wise land-use laws. The club took on the preservation of Yellowstone National Park, which had been formed in 1872 but which continued to be ravaged by poachers, timber cutters, vandals and trappers, as one of its first projects. Since that time, the Boone and Crockett Club has supported many major conservation moves in the U.S.

The first record book, *Records Of North American Big Game*, was published in 1932. Since that time the scoring system has been revised extensively, and a number of updated record books have been published. Now Boone and Crockett trophy entry periods run for three years, and at the end of each scoring period, a banquet is held to honor trophies entered during the three-year period. Boone and Crockett publishes revised versions of *Records Of North American Big Game* periodically. Each revision normally covers two scoring periods, or six years.

Boone and Crockett records are open to any North American big game trophy, as long as the animal meets the minimum established score. Trophies taken by any fair chase method (modern firearm, bow, muzzleloader, handgun) are eligible for entry.

For more information on the Boone and Crockett Club and its records-keeping program contact:

Boone & Crockett Club
241 S. Fraley Blvd.
Dumfries, VA 22026
(703) 221-1888

Pope and Young Club. The bowhunter's equivalent of Boone and Crockett is the Pope and Young Club. During the first half of the 20th Century, bowhunting was viewed askance by many hunters and wildlife managers, as some sort of gimmick for hunting fanatics but certainly not as a serious form of hunting. Many archers believed a serious organization similar to the Boone and Crockett Club was needed to give bowhunting credibility, and as a result, on January 27, 1961, Glenn St. Charles, an avid big game hunter from Seattle, Washington, and some of his bowhunting associates, formally established the Pope and Young Club. The club derives its name from Dr. Saxton Pope and Art Young, dedicated archers who hunted around the world during the 1920s and who were largely responsible for launching bowhunting out of the dark ages into the modern hunting era.

The Pope and Young Club now holds an awards program and banquet every two years. Top trophies entered during the biennium are measured by a panel of judges and displayed at the banquet. Pope and Young published its first record book, *Bowhunting Big Game Records Of North America*, in 1975, and revised editions are published every few years.

For more information about the Pope and Young Club, contact:

Pope and Young Club
Box 548
Chatfield, MN 55923
(507) 867-4144

A Final Thought On Trophy Hunting

Not all hunters are interested in trophy hunting. Simply killing an elk of any size satisfies the hunting desires of many hunters. But after a person has taken a certain number of elk, he may crave to renew the challenge of hunting by voluntarily placing obstacles in his own path to make the hunting more difficult and to extend the time he can spend in the field.

Trophy hunting is one way to do these things. By passing up smaller animals, a hunter can spend more time hunting without killing any more game. Many detractors cry that trophy hunters hurt game herds by taking the prime animals. In a sense that may be true, but the person who really holds out for nothing but the biggest animals actually makes a much smaller impact on elk herds than the hunter driven to fill a tag year after year.

Trophy hunting demands control—control to avoid pulling the trigger or releasing an arrow when an average bull presents an easy shot. It's often said that you'll never kill a trophy bull if you shoot the first spike that comes along, and maybe that's the central axiom for trophy-hunting success. You simply must hold out, and if you crave to fill a tag, you'll have a hard time ever killing trophy bulls.

Because that's true, a trophy elk hunter must be content to return home empty handed, not only occasionally but frequently. The person who will succeed at trophy hunting must have a strong self image, and he or she must be the kind of person who doesn't need the approval of others. If you worry about what others will think if you don't fill a tag, you won't succeed in trophy hunting, because you'll continue to fill tags with lesser bulls. A dedicated trophy hunter must feel comfortable in failure, satisfied in knowing he's done his best and that he didn't sell out his principles just to kill an elk.

Perhaps that philosophy contributes more to successful trophy hunting than knowledge of equipment, hunting areas, antler-judging ability, or any other aspect of hunting. It's the very basis for taking big bulls.

And it points out why trophy hunters have less impact on game herds than the throngs of average hunters. They kill less game. But they're content with killing less because they have only themselves to satisfy, and when they take the animal of their dreams, their satisfaction is great.

Elk hunting is Duane Wiltse's livelihood. You can learn a lot from a man whose knowledge has been gained in elk hunting's school of hard knocks.

12

Through The Eyes
Of An Elk Guide

Elk are the most naturally alert big game animal in North America. A bull's ability to protect himself in his natural environment is phenomenal.

For every elk you see, half a dozen or more have melted into the surrounding cover, undetected. Some years ago, I was leading a moose hunting party into Wyoming's Thorofare country. The horse trail winds through timbered hills and grassy meadows for 40 miles. It is excellent elk habitat. Enroute, we camped overnight and the next morning we broke camp at dawn to begin the final leg of our journey. Twenty minutes out of camp, my eldest son, Mark, flew over our pack string in a Piper Super Cub. Ten days later, when we returned home with a big bull moose, Mark asked me if I had seen all of the elk we were pushing in front of us that morning. From the air, he had seen an estimated 40 to 60 head of elk fanning out on three sides of us, either secretly watching us or sneaking away. The four of us on horseback never knew they were there!

The first step in hunting elk successfully is to hunt where the elk are. The West's hunting country is vast. There may be miles and miles of beautiful country between the proper habitat. Elk frequent different parts of their domain at different times of the year and even at different times of the day.

From mid-September to mid-October, the normal bugling season, you will usually find the elk high. By high I mean just at or above timberline. They are still on their summer range. Lone bulls travel from one drainage to another, bugling and looking for cows, or a fight, or both. At that time of year, when they are bugling and on the move, bulls are most susceptible to mistakes. I think everyone should experience a bugle hunt, but it is by no means the best or last word in elk hunting. It is an unpredictable time to hunt and it's next to impossible to judge what a bull will do. Sometimes this unpredictability works to a hunter's advantage and sometimes to his demise.

I remember leaving camp an hour and a half before sunrise on a clear, sharp October morning. Two hours of steady climbing on horseback took us from the camp elevation of 7,500 feet to a beautiful secluded basin at 10,000 feet. A bull was bugling from the timber at the lower end of the basin as my father, my son and an NAHC member on his first elk hunt and I rode into the upper end of the basin.

After watching cows, calves and a proud, majestic 6-point bull filter around and through the timber below us for over half an hour, a plan of action was formed.

We had two problems to solve. The elk were too far away to shoot at accurately because of their grazing activities in the sparse timber. Secondly, our club member had asthma and simply could not travel very far or very fast afoot in that kind of terrain and altitude.

We had entered the basin along the elks' upper escape route, had hidden our horses in some timber and were ourselves screened by rocks and juniper. We decided our hunter was in as good a place as possible to make his stand. By circling, I could move quietly into position below the elk so that my scent would put them out past our hidden hunter. A man's scent will move elk more surely than sight or sound will.

I was half way to where I wanted to get when I realized the bull was moving steadily downhill and away from my hunter. I was keeping track of the bull by his bugling and there was no doubt about it, he was moving downhill. The cows would be in front of him and probably some of the leaders would be almost as low as me already. I knew my only hope was to cut them off before they entered the black timber below the basin and holed up for the day.

I broke into a run. Nothing to lose now, I thought. In fact, I wanted the elk to know I was down there. After about a 60-yard sprint, I burst into the thin stretch of timber that the elk were traveling down. Sure enough, there were several cows and calves just above me. None had gotten by yet. I hollered and waved my arms at them. They all stopped in sudden surprise. None of them moved. We were less than 10 yards from each other, eyeball to eyeball. I fired two shots into the air and they all turned back towards the bull. I figured when they got back to the bull they would all use the upper escape route, providing my hunter with an excellent shooting opportunity.

Wrong! I had hardly caught my breath before they came back. The bull had made it plain to them that they were going where he wanted to go. The lead cow was going to pass about 20 yards in front of me. She approached deliberately and hesitated for a moment. There were approximately 18 cows and calves strung out behind her.

I knew it was my last chance to turn them, so I pulled on a rock about five yards in front of her and squeezed off a shot. The rock exploded, the cow snorted and trotted right through there anyway. The bull bugled again and the rest of the cows and calves followed the lead cow. Shortly after that, the bull appeared. . .a majestic monarch of the high country with heavy sweeping horns that rocked to and fro with each challenging step. He had six perfectly matched points per side with a unique flare in each beam about a foot from the end. He stopped closer to me than the cow had been; maybe 10 yards away.

Again I raised my old Model 94 Winchester, the rifle that had been passed on to me from my grandfather. A rock about 10 yards in front of the bull exploded from the impact of the 150-grain soft-nose bullet. He didn't move a muscle! I levered the .32 Special again. Still no movement from the bull. When I fired my last shot, stone chips and mud exploded no more than 10 feet in front of the bull. Still no retreat. The bull glared at me as I reloaded my rifle. Not knowing anything better to do, I took my hat off to him as he trotted past me shaking his horns and bugling after his cows.

Another time, I was hurrying to post my hunter on a strategic vantage point of a dog-legged meadow surrounded by timber. I wanted to have him there at daybreak, but the steep climb over downed timber and 8,000 feet elevation had taken its toll on him in the first quarter mile out of camp. The sun was rapidly displacing the shade and crisp air when we finally arrived. The lateness of the hour, it was between 8:30 and 9:00 a.m., had me somewhat frustrated and irritable.

As we reached the near side of the meadow, by way of a well-used elk trail, I was not surprised to find the grassy feeding ground empty. But until we reached the point in the dog leg, we couldn't be sure that there weren't some late feeders around the bend. We had just started into the open when, some distance away, a bull bugled from the timber beyond. We had taken only a few more steps when he bugled again, somewhat closer but still a fair piece off. With some urgency now, we hurried to reach the stand about 60 yards away in the hope that the bull might expose himself along the opposite timberline. But we never had a chance! Moments later he bugled again, this time not more than 50 yards inside the opposing timber. We were on a collision course. We were using the same trail!

The bull had all the advantages except one; he didn't know we were there. We were caught out in the open, but he wasn't paying as much attention as he should have been. Clamping my hand on my hunter's shoulder, I whispered hoarsely, "Sit down and be still!"

By the time I had jerked his shiny new blaze orange hat off his head and sat on it, (I sure hate shiny new hats and noisy coats or pants. You just can't beat wool!) I could see massive antlers threading their way through the timber towards us. The bull burst into the meadow, using no caution, not checking for danger or slipping around the edges. He was grunting, squealing, pawing the dirt and throwing his head. He was less than 75 yards away and madder than hell. He had just been whipped by another bull and was looking for someone to whip himself. He was bleeding from tine wounds in his neck and ribs and his five, big, sharp, ivory tines were covered with the blood of his opponent. I know the bull that had whipped him . . . a monster weighing between 950 and 1,000 pounds with a 35 cow harem, seven points on one side and eight on the other and ivory plumb to his hindquarters. But he's another story.

I was having trouble containing myself because the hunter had passed up what I considered to be two or three of the best opportunities for good killing shots. When he finally shot, the bull wheeled and disappeared in the timber he had just emerged from. Much to the hunter's dismay, I insisted that we sit perfectly still and be quiet for 15 minutes. Then I further frustrated him by insisting that he stay put while I quietly circled around well above where the bull had disappeared, and I sneaked down into the timber for a closer look.

The hunter was sure the bull was dead and I certainly hoped so, but he had nothing to lose and a fine trophy bull to gain by being careful. Sure enough, 15 minutes later as I wormed my way to the right spot, I spotted the bull laying with his head up, watching his back track, sick, but ready to bolt at the first sign of being followed. He never heard Grandad's old .32 Special crack.

There are an endless array of stories to be told about elk's unpredictability during the rut. Don't plan on an easy hunt or an easy bull. Those are pipe dreams. You must hunt for the proper habitat, for the time of year you are hunting, and then hunt for your elk in that vicinity. I believe that the results will be at least as satisfying and far more predictable if time honored and proven methods are employed, such as posting, glassing, stalking, tracking, etc.

A good, solid, positive attitude is worth more than all the sporting goods store gadgets you can buy. Take time for your senses to adjust and appreciate the new environment. Listen to what Mother Nature has to tell you and see what she has to show you.

Elk simply will not adjust their habits and behavior patterns to fit your 9:00 to 5:00 schedule. Generally speaking, elk feed at night and lay down during the day. I believe that the first two hours of daylight and the last hour of light at night are worth more than the rest of the hours in a day put together. This means that you will need to get up by 4:00 a.m. to be out of camp an hour or two before dawn.

In order to be sharp and alert for the evening hours, most hunters need some rest in the middle of the day. So don't feel guilty about taking a nap because that's what most of the game animals are doing too. Depending on the weather, from 11:00 a.m. until 4:00 p.m., there is very little if anything moving, especially if the weather is warm. So if you are posting that day, build a small fire, toast your sandwich, then take a nap. The relaxing change of pace for a few hours will contribute to aggressive alertness on your part that evening.

If for some reason the decision is made to change posting locations or drainages, that change should naturally be made during the middle of the day, leaving at least an hour for things to settle down and return to normal before you can expect elk to begin their evening grazing.

Posting and glassing are by far the most productive ways of hunting elk. They can be boring when nothing is moving, but are more successful by far than any other methods you can employ.

I had a hunter posted on a knob in the middle of Swede Creek drainage where over the years we have seen and shot a lot of elk. My hunter intently swept his watering eyes back and forth over the panorama that lay before us. The rising sun caused the shadows to retreat into the patches of black timber scattered throughout our field of vision, revealing no elk.

While the hunter was watching everything within rifle range, I had taken advantage of the increasing light to glass some small secluded meadows at the head of the drainage. Suddenly, the sun flashed off the yellow side of an elk a mile away. As I watched, I thought I saw sun reflecting off his ivory tipped antlers as he grazed slowly into the last small patch of timber just below the jumble of rocks and boulders that extended to the top of the mountain.

We maintained our vigil on both locations until around 10:00 a.m. Not hearing or seeing anything, we made plans to lay siege to the elk that I had seen disappear in yonder timber. Of course, by now we had not only built him up to be a bull, but a big 6-point bull as well. Between us and the "big bull" were a number of deep canyons that prevented travel by horseback. So, tying our heavy clothing to our saddles and pocketing sandwiches, knives and hatchets, we struck out, full of hope and energy. Needless to say, our hopes lasted longer than our energy. By the time we had climbed up to that little meadow, it was about 3:00 p.m.

Our hope was waivering, and I was being threatened by the hunter with all kinds of mayhem if the elk was not at least a legal bull. Because it would be practically impossible to find our way back to our horses in the dark, we could not afford the luxury of waiting in ambush for our bull to begin his evening feeding. We settled on a plan whereby the hunter would guard the most likely escape route from the patch of timber and I would flush the elk out of his bed.

When everything was set, I entered the timber. Two shots later, the hunter bagged a nice 4-point bull. It was "dark-thirty" when we reached camp that night, but that is what you must be prepared for when you hunt elk. We had had a day of applying excellent hunting skills that we both will long remember.

When you are posting, use as much protection and cover as the natural terrain will allow. Stay off the skyline and get out of the wind as much as possible. Provide a rest for your rifle.

Keep your horse hidden and some distance away from you. Some horses tend to be fidgety and noisy when separated from their traveling companions, so you may have to tie two or three of them near each other to prevent a lot of whinnying.

It works very well to have a buddy with you. There are a lot more options available to a pair of hunters than to a single hunter. If you are hunting an area that lends itself to driving timbered draws or aspen groves, a party of hunters working together will have far more success than a lone hunter will. Just keep in mind the wind currents and use them to your advantage. You can rest assured that the elk are using them and they will use the wind currents against you if you let them.

On a frosty fall morning, my clients, a pair of brothers, and I shiveringly awaited the sun's warming rays from that same knob in Swede Creek drainage. We had hidden our horses on the opposite side and were just below the skyline, screened by a little clump of Ponderosa pines. We had only been there a few minutes when a cow and calf materialized from the timber below and to the left of us. The wind was in our favor and the elk nonchalantly grazed along the ridge trail right at us.

About the time the pair reached the base of the knob, about 25 yards away, a big 5-point bull emerged from the timber and came down the ridge toward us just like the cow and calf had. He was no more than 75 yards away when he first appeared, closing fast. But no one was shooting. The cow and calf were too close for me to say anything to my hunters! The bull kept coming.

The cow and calf turned and began grazing to our right, about 15 yards off the trail. I realized then that the hunters were waiting for the bull to follow suit and give them a broadside shot at him. But I figure when the apple is ripe, it is time to pick it! There had been too many good shots passed up waiting for him to turn and something unexpected was bound to happen this time, I thought. Sure enough, as the bull swung his head to turn, following the same route the cow and calf had taken, mama wapiti laid back her ears and charged the bull. One jump put him back over the ridge and into cover with only a foot of his horns waving to and fro as he jogged downhill and out of sight.

After the two disbelieving hunters came to their senses, I repositioned one of them behind a large rock outcropping, giving him a perfect rest for aiming and a different field of view. I thought if I could get below and around the bull and give him my scent from the right angle, he would likely bolt back across the ridge and follow the cow and calf.

I got lucky! Shortly there commenced such a cannonading that you would have thought someone was trying to steal our horses. By the time I reached the scene of the crime, the hunters were gazing wistfully off into the distance. They were a sorry-looking pair, with dejected expressions on their faces, and eight or 10 empty shell casings at their feet. When I asked what had happened, they hesitated and then the older brother brightened and said, "At least we stood the s.o.b. off, Duane. He never was able to take this knob and breed your horses!"

We all had a good laugh, but the point is that sometimes you can use your scent against a bull instead of him using it against you.

There are several things you can do to mask your scent. First, be aware that dark complexions are usually more oily than light complexions, thereby giving off more scent. But your own human scent is far less detectable than the odor left by the soap that you bathe with. Antiperspirants, after-shave lotions, shaving creams, colognes or perfumes really broadcast your presence. The two things that I have found to work well for me are wood smoke or apples. It is quite easy to take on the aroma of a campfire by getting smoke and ashes on your hands, boots and clothing. Eating an apple and squeezing a few drops of the juice on your hands and clothing is another excellent method of camouflaging the human scent. While elk are not accustomed to apple orchards like many deer may be, the smell of apples is a pleasant and enticing thing to them, it seems.

One of my favorite methods of hunting elk is pussyfooting around the edge of meadows, along game trails or through open timbered slopes during a drizzling rain. I mentioned earlier in this chapter that the middle of the day isn't worth much. You realize, I am sure, that weather patterns and terrain should dictate the hunting technique. I will take a cloudy, threatening drizzly day over bright sunshine for bringing down bull elk anytime. Unfortunately, most elk hunters are locked into a certain time period dictated by the calendar and cannot choose the weather that they would prefer to hunt in. Being aware of the weather and changing weather patterns is all a part of getting tuned in to the surrounding environment. Don't sit around and complain about the lousy weather. Be flexible; employ skills and techniques that current circumstances call for. Elk are active during light, drizzling rain. Get out there and get on them! You've got all year to dry out!

Another favorite method of mine is to track elk on fresh snow. Any snow is better than no snow, but I would rather hunt elk on fresh snow than any other way, including bugling. The snow takes away the background that elk blend into so easily and makes them easier to see. In my estimation, tracking a bull in fresh snow is a great way to spend a day, whether you see him or not. You will need to forget everything else and immerse yourself in the game of hide-and-seek. You can't be thinking about the troublesome teenager at home or the things you didn't get done at the office before you left home. You can study those projects while you are posting. Now you must pay attention to the little details in and around his tracks that not only tell you what the bull has done, but more importantly, what he may do. You can't always guess right of course, but when you do, the sense of accomplishment is second to none.

If you are going to track elk successfully, you can't look or sound like a walking sporting goods store with the last word in paraphernalia hanging all over you. You must travel light and be light-footed. Know the country well enough that you can close out all concern except how to get close enough, quietly enough to get a shot at this bull.

After cutting a track, it must be qualified. Is it fresh enough to bother with? How is the elk traveling? Has he been spooked? Is he travelling cross country, or is he wandering aimlessly along, nibbling and smelling things? Was the track made by a cow or is it a bull? Of course you will have to study the track for a few yards to gain answers to these questions. . .maybe as much as a half mile. Then be realistic about your conclusion. If it is not a bull, wishing won't change anything.

Weather, like wind, and snow conditions must be taken into consideration when determining the freshness of a track. Compare it to your own tracks for contrast. A thawing day can make a 30 minute-old track look like it is a day old. In fresh, powdery snow, the direction the elk is going may be difficult to determine. The way he drags his toes is the key in that case. The thin end of the mark indicates the direction he is coming from.

If the elk has been spooked or if you spook him, he will be on the alert and covering country as only an elk can. You have only two chances of seeing him that day...slim and none!

Some hunters will mistake a cow with a calf for a bull and a cow. There are a lot of cows that will make a track as big or bigger than some bulls. Calves can weigh as much as 300 pounds in November and leave tracks that look enticing to the normal whitetail hunter. I seldom follow anything but a large, lone track and more times than I care to admit, it has turned out to be an old dry cow, living alone.

Remember, cows squat and splash when they urinate. When bulls urinate, they leave a round hole in the snow. Bulls also beat up little pine trees. Sometimes a bull will lay down and get up two or three times in his travels before he is satisfied and stops for the day. You may be able to see the faint imprint of his antlers left in the snow near these beds.

Again, weather plays a vital role in what an elk is likely to do, so you must adjust your approach accordingly. If it is a warm, sunny day, and you pick up a fresh track in the morning, the elk is likely heading for his "hidey-hole" to lay down for the day. He will approach his bedding area from a circular route so that he can lay out of sight and watch his backtrack at the same time. He will select a spot that offers his two vital components to survival...a view of any approaching danger and an escape route that is one jump over the backside of the bed and out of sight. So on a warm, sunny day, your best bet (if you didn't catch up to him before he lays down) is to pick up a fresh track in late afternoon, after the elk has gotten out of his bed for the day and is beginning to graze.

Stormy weather makes for a different set of rules. If a storm is short in duration, then the elk are active. But when snowfall amounts are heavy and the storm is more than one day in duration, the elk hole up in heavy timber, out of the storm. The first day after such a snow storm, good hunting conditions prevail because elk are very active for the entire day.

One of the most satisfying hunts I have ever had was after just such a heavy snow. We had about five inches of fresh snow, the day was warm and thawing. At about 9:00 in the morning, I picked up a lone track that was nearly as fresh as mine. I was in the flat bottom of a large timbered draw. I followed the track only about 50 yards when it led me to a four-inch pine tree that had been rubbed and shredded by sharp antlers. That really got my attention! Yet I thought that my chances of seeing the elk were very slim because while the scattered, bushy pines gave him good cover, they had no limbs from knee-high down. Perfect for a grazing bull's eyes to catch the movement of my feet before I could see him. After two hours of this kind of cover, the bull moved off the bottom of the draw to the heavier timber on one of the small ridges above it. This gave me the hope of picking up the pace and closing on him from behind one of the small hills. I eased just my head over each hill and studied the other side for several minutes, then quietly I moved over, down and up the next hill. Several hours and many hills later as I peeked over a downed tree, there he was as big as life. I think we saw each other simultaneously. I was taught how to hunt using a single shot .22 and then promoted to a single shot shotgun and I have always gotten my share of the meat and this day was no exception. I only wanted one shot. I made it when the apple was ripe.

But meat is not meat until it is in the pot, and I had lost all sense of time and direction while concentrating on the stalk.

After I field dressed the elk and protected the meat from birds, I walked down the draw to the river and into camp. I planned to pack out my meat the next morning.

The next day, the terrain made it necessary to use a different route for getting the pack string into the kill site and that night, another six inches of new snow had fallen, changing the appearance of everything. I hunted high and low for nearly an hour and still couldn't find my bull. Then I cut a coyote track trotting in a straight line. Coyotes don't travel in straight lines. "That bandit is heading for my meat," I thought to myself. Another 15 minutes of coyote tracking brought me to my once-killed and twice-tracked 5-point bull. I lost the liver to the coyote, but added a nice coyote pelt to my trophy room.

It is always best to mark your kill site and a route to it well. I had a pair of hunters from Wisconsin stray off by themselves one evening and kill a nice 6-point bull elk. I was just leaving camp to look for them when they returned at dusk, happy and excited about their good fortune. They assured me that they had marked the site of the kill and their route well enough to be easily found the next morning by using fluorescent surveyor's tape. And by golly, they were right! The elk was a cinch to find the next day when our packers went out. I untied all of the ribbons and put them in my pocket as we went by. I hate to leave anything in the woods but tracks, but I like the ribbon idea because they can be seen easily in any kind of weather, are easily applied and removed with no damage to the environment such as blazed trees or broken limbs.

There is a lot of luck connected to successful elk hunting the same as there is in hunting any species, such as being in the right place at the right time, making a difficult shot, etc. And luck puts a lot of meat on the table, but deep down inside every hunter, the sense of accomplishment, the feeling of pride, is far more profound if his success was brought about largely by his own patience and hunting skills.

Enjoy the hunt and remember that just as application of basic discipline and skills leads to success in other aspects of life, the same is true of elk hunting. After all, the value of hunting is in the hunt, not the kill. The value is in communing with nature in the very basic way that only hunting provides; the competition with game and elements alike; the solitude, excitement, adventure and camaraderie experienced only while hunting; and most importantly what you can learn about yourself. You can buy a lot of expensive counseling and not find out as much about yourself as you can in 10 days in the high country, hunting elk, listening to ravens and watching eagles soar.

When you embark on an elk hunt, you are in for the most challenging and potentially rewarding experience of your life. There is nothing second class about a bull elk or the country he inhabits. From the vast, sweeping and awe inspiring vistas of the high country to the barking cows, to the proud bugling challenge of the bulls, it's first class all the way.

Index